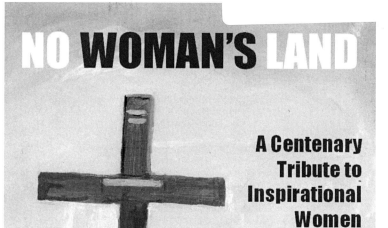

NO WOMAN'S LAND

A Centenary
Tribute to
Inspirational
Women
Of
World
War
One

Compiled By Lucy London

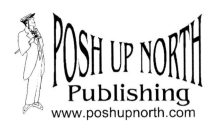

First published in Great Britain in 2014 by
Posh Up North Publishing
Blackpool FY4 1EG/4

British Library cataloguing in publication data.
A catalogue record for this book is available from the British Library

Print Version: ISBN 978-1-909643-07-9

Download Version: ISBN 978-1-909643-08-6

Front Cover Image: "Grave Of An Unknown Soldier" by Mary Riter Hamilton – courtesy of Archives Canada

Back Cover Image: "Filling In Shell Holes In No Mans Land" by Mary Riter Hamilton – Courtesy of Archives Canada

CONTENTS

My paternal grandmother Lucy Mary Uffindell
pictured on a Bank Holiday outing circa 1901
(Photo by Arthur John Condon)

INTRODUCTION

"The only way to prove that women can do this, that or the other with success is to go and do it". M.A. St. Clair Stobart (1862 – 1954)

In the Spring of 2012, I began researching women who wrote poetry during the First World War for an exhibition at The Wilfred Owen Story museum in Argyle Street, Birkenhead, Wirral (UK). In putting together the exhibition in memory of my Grandfather who was an "Old Contemptible", and my Great Uncle, who was killed at Arras in April 1917, I tried to highlight the global impact of the conflict and to show that women took a much more active part than is generally accepted.

As my research continued, I found many women who were not poets – women like Mary Riter Hamilton, the Canadian artist who went to France in 1919 to paint the aftermath – and I just could not leave them out. I therefore created two more sections – Inspirational Women of World War One and Fascinating Facts of the Great War.

The Balkan Wars gave women like Mrs. Mabel St. Clair Stobart, whose words at the top of this Introduction have become my motto and who founded The Women's Sick and Wounded Convoy Corps in 1912, and many other women, among them Kathleen Scott the sculptress, a chance to help out in a practical way in a war zone.

At the time of the First World War, Victorian values were still very much in evidence in Britain – God, the reigning monarch, the family, duty, honour, obedience, patriotic pride and so on were of supreme importance to everyone.

Until the First World War, women had traditionally wielded the distaff (i.e. the work of spinning, weaving, milking cows and so on). After the Industrial Revolution, many women worked in factories, as pit brow lassies, as domestic servants and as governesses and school teachers. However, there were many who did not work. Women did not have the right to vote and were very much 'second class citizens' – hence the efforts of the Suffragettes. It was widely believed that women's brains would explode if attempts were made to educate them. This is the background to the situation of women as World War One began.

Anne Powell tells us that over 46,000 British women went to help out during the conflict. According to Joshua Goldstein in his book "War and Gender: How Gender Shapes The War System And Vice Versa", more than 25,000 American women travelled to Europe to help out as doctors, nurses, clerks, entertainers and to run refreshment stands and so on.

Women from other countries answered the call for help - Canada, Newfoundland, Australia, New Zealand and South Africa and the countries of the Axis Powers also had women helpers, some of whom fought. There were also British women - for instance Flora Sandes from East Anglia - who fought. Women were present in many theatres of the conflict and it is all too easy for us to forget in modern times, especially when visiting the immaculate cemeteries of the Commonwealth War Graves Commission, the conditions under which those women worked and lived.

Many of those wonderful, inspirational women died in service and are buried far from their homes. If you think women just stayed at home to keep the home fires burning during WW1, think again.

I hope the women you will meet in this volume will inspire you to follow Mrs Stobart's suggestion. And I hope you will join me in commemorating all those whose lives have been affected through conflict anywhere in the world with honour, respect and dignity.

Don't forget to plant poppy seeds in remembrance.

Lucy London, October 2014

MABEL ANNIE St CLAIR STOBART
English Adventurer & Aid Pioneer
(1862 - 1954)

Mabel Annie Boulton was born on 3rd February 1862 in Woolwich, the daughter of Sir Samuel Bagster Boulton and Sophia Louisa Cooper.

She married St. Clair Kelburn Stobart, a granite merchant on 16th July 1884. The couple lived in Cornwall for seven years and had two children. They then moved to London and in 1903 - after some financial difficulties – went to run a farm in a remote area of the Transvaal.

They decided to return to England in 1907 with Mabel travelling first and her husband to follow afterwards. Unfortunately, he died on the way back from Africa.

Upon her return to in England in 1907, London was in the midst of a war scare – with fears of a German invasion.

Mabel realised that women were poorly prepared in the event of an invasion and would achieve the vote only if they could demonstrate their ability to aid in the defence of the nation.

Mabel joined the First Aid Nursing Yeomanry Corps – so called because its members were on horseback and provided a link between Field Hospitals and the Front Lines where troops were fighting.

However, she decided to establish her own service, the Women's Sick and Wounded Convoy Corps, which was intended to facilitate the movement of the wounded from the field hospitals to the base hospitals in the rear. After a three-year period of training, the Corps saw its first service in the First Balkan War of 1912-13, in aid of the Bulgarian Army.

The experiences of the unit demonstrated that women could not only be efficient war-time nurses but also surgeons, doctors, orderlies, administrators, drivers and interpreters. Mabel's book "Women and War", published by G. Bell & Sons, London, 1913, told the world of the unit's experiences in Bulgaria. In his "Prefatory Note" to the book, Viscount Esher says "… it is impossible to resist Mrs Stobart's plea for the reconsideration of the place assigned to women in the scheme of National Defence."

Mrs Stobart was rather scathing in her criticism of the Red Cross Voluntary Aid Detachment scheme, which she felt "played with women" and both she and Viscount Esher resigned their membership of the British Red Cross for that reason.

On 5th August 1914 – the day after war was declared – with the help of Lady Muir McKenzie, Mabel founded the Women's National Service League with the aim of providing a body of women qualified to give service at home or abroad. This included women doctors, trained nurses, cooks, interpreters, and all workers essential for the independent working of a hospital of war

She offered the services of a women's medical unit to the Belgian Red Cross and travelled to Brussels to set up a hospital in the University buildings. The following day, the Germans entered the city, took over the Belgian Croix Rouge and commandeered the hospital for their own use.   Mrs Stobart escaped to Tongres where she was arrested and condemned to death as a spy. When she remonstrated with the Major in charge, he replied "You are English and this is a War of annihilation". (page 8 "The Flaming Sword".)

Mabel managed to escape and returned to England where she re-organised the unit and offered their services to the French who asked her to set up a hospital in Cherbourg. After four months of treating wounded soldiers in France, Mrs Stobart heard that a typhus epidemic in Serbia meant they needed urgent medical care so she offered her services to the Serbian Relief Fund and organised a hospital in Serbia.

Mabel served as a commissioned major in charge of a hospital column during the three-month retreat on the Balkan Front and, despite being fifty-three at the time, spent eighteen hours a day on horseback in the mountains in winter conditions.

After her return from the Balkans, Mabel published an account of her war-time adventures in 1916 under the title "The Flaming Sword in Serbia and Elsewhere" and, later, an autobiography called "Miracles And Adventures" in 1935. She travelled and gave an extensive series of lectures both in Britain and in the United States and, in later life, became an ardent Spiritualist.

By her own account, Mabel must have been a prolific writer because she refers to one of her plays being performed at a fund-raising charity event in Cherbourg.

Mabel died in Bournemouth, on 7th December 1954 aged 93.

Sources: http://ghgraham.org/stclairstobart1861.html
http://www.gutenberg.org/files/43124/43124-h/43124-h.htm
https://archive.org/details/warwomenfromexpe00stobrich
"The Flaming Sword in Serbia and Elsewhere" published by Hodder and Stoughton, London, 1916
"War and Women", published by G. Bell & Sons, Ltd., London, 1913.

"THE LADY OF THE BLACK HORSE" (Mrs. St. Clair Stobart)
During the Serbian Retreat, October-December, 1915 painted by George Rankin
Taken from "The Flaming Sword in Serbia and Elsewhere"

ELIZABETH GARRETT ANDERSON
English Doctor & Feminist
(1836 - 1917)

"...a doctor leads two lives - the professional and the private - and the boundaries between the two are never traversed." Elizabeth Garrett Anderson (Manton, Jo.- "Elizabeth Garrett Anderson: England's First Woman Physician"- Methuen, London, 1965)

Elizabeth was born on 9th June 1836 in Whitechapel, London. Her parents were Newson and Louisa Garrett (née Dunnell). In 1841, the family moved to Aldeburgh in Suffolk (East Anglia, England) where they lived opposite the church until 1852.

Elizabeth's father had purchased a barley malting and coal merchant business in nearby Snape. By 1850 the business had grown sufficiently for Newson to be able to build Alde House, a mansion just outside the town.

Since there was no school in Aldeburgh at that time, Elizabeth's early education was from her mother until a governess was engaged to teach the Garrett children when Elizabeth was ten years old. When she was thirteen, Elizabeth was sent to a boarding school in Blackheath, London run by Robert Browning's aunt, Louisa Browning.

In 1859 Elizabeth joined the Society for Promoting the Employment of Women and, following a meeting with Emily Davies - feminist and co-founder of Girton College, Cambridge - she decided to train as a doctor.

The path of her chosen career was a steep one, in spite of her father's total support. Initial opposition meant that Elizabeth first had to train as a nurse at Middlesex Hospital. She then studied anatomy and physiology with a private tutor and eventually was allowed to join dissecting and chemistry lectures at the Hospital.

Her presence, however, was not welcomed by her fellow male students and she was eventually forced to leave. Applications to medical schools in Oxford, Cambridge, Glasgow, Edinburgh, St. Andrews and the Royal College of Surgeons were turned down so Elizabeth obtained a certificate in anatomy and physiology after which she was accepted by the Society of Apothecaries to study privately.

Elizabeth studied privately with some of the most noted professors of the day from the University of St. Andrews, the Edinburgh Royal Maternity Hospital and the London Hospital Medical School. In 1865, she took her final examination and obtained a licence from the Society of Apothecaries to practise medicine, becoming the first woman in the UK to quality as a doctor and obtaining the highest marks of any of the students. The Society thereupon changed their regulations in order to prevent other women obtaining a licence.

In spite of her qualifications, Elizabeth was not permitted to work as a doctor in any hospital so she opened her own practice at 20 Upper Berkeley Street, London. In 1865 during a cholera epidemic, Elizabeth's prowess as a doctor won her the respect of her 3,000 patients.

When Elizabeth heard that the Dean of the University of Sorbonne in Paris had agreed to allow women to study medicine, she learnt French specially so that she could enroll. She finally obtained a degree from the Sorbonne in 1870.

In 1871, Elizabeth married James George Skelton Anderson whose uncle owned the Orient Steamship Company. Her husband must have been very pro married women working because Elizabeth was allowed to continue her career. The couple had three children, one of whom – Louisa (1873 – 1943) - became a doctor and feminist activist.

In 1873, Elizabeth became a member of the British Medical Association and was the only woman member for over nineteen years. Elizabeth worked hard to develop the New Hospital for Women and in 1874 created the London School of Medicine for Women, serving as Dean. She also championed the cause of women's rights, joining the British Women's Suffrage Committee. After the death of her husband in 1907, Elizabeth travelled extensively with some of the younger members of her extended family.

Elizabeth was elected Mayor of Aldeburgh on 9th November 1908 – the first woman to hold the post of Mayor in England. She died in 1917 and is buried in Aldeburgh.

The New Hospital for Women was renamed the "Elizabeth Garrett Anderson Hospital" in 1918 in her memory and amalgamated with the Obstetric Hospital in 2001 to form the Elizabeth Garrett Anderson and Obstetric Hospital before moving and becoming The University College Hospital Elizabeth Garrett Anderson Wing at UCH in London.

She was commemorated on a postage stamp in 2008 (see below).

EDITH CAVELL
English Nurse
(1865 – 1915)

Edith Cavell was one of my childhood heroines – her courage was outstanding and her brilliance as a nurse needs recording.

Edith was born on 4th December 1865 in Swardeston, near Norwich, Norfolk. Her Father, the Reverend Frederick Cavell, was the Anglican Vicar of the parish for 45 years. Edith was the eldest of four children. She worked as a governess in Brussels in Belgium from 1900 until 1905 before returning to England to become a nurse, training at the London Hospital.

In 1907, Edith was taken on by Dr. Antoine Depage as matron of a new nursing school in Brussels. By 1910, she was in charge of training for three hospitals, twenty-four schools and thirteen kindergartens in Belgium.

When war was declared in 1914, Edith was visiting her mother. She returned to Belgium, where her clinic and nursing school had been taken over by the Red Cross.

After the German occupation of Belgium, Edith began to shelter British soldiers and help them to escape. She was helped in this work by Prince Reginald de Croy who had a large estate and stately home at Belignie near Mons.

The Germans became increasingly suspicious of the coming and going of large numbers of men at the hospital in Brussels and Edith's frankness did not help matters. She was arrested on 3rd August 1915 and charged with hiding Allied soldiers, which was considered to be treason. She was held in St. Gilles prison, tried and shot on 12th October 1915.

Following Edith's execution, her story spread across the world. She became a heroine and her story was used to recruit soldiers and sell war bonds. Her death was presented as a German act of brutality and moral depravity and inspired songs, poems, and – later on – plays and films.

In the words of the German Army chaplain who attended Edith prior to her execution "Miss Cavell was a very brave woman and a faithful Christian."

At that time, women were not considered capable of the courage and stoicism that Edith demonstrated and this brought her even greater acclaim than a man in similar circumstances would have received.

Edith Cavell's memory lives on in many ways throughout the world.

LE PLUS GRAND
CRIME DES BARBARES
Hommage à Miss Cavell.

LE MARTYRE DE MISS CAVELL
ASSASSINÉE PAR LES ALLEMANDS
Complainte d'Actualité.　　　　　Air : La Palmpolaise.

NELLIE SPINDLER
English Nursing Sister
(1891 – 1917)

Nellie was born in Wakefield, Yorkshire in 1891. Her parents were George and Elizabeth Spindler. George was an inspector with the Yorkshire police.

Nellie trained as a nurse and in 1914 she joined The Queen Alexandra's Imperial Military Nursing Service (formed in 1902). In 1914 there were 3,000 nurses assigned to the BEF. By 1918 this number had risen to 23,000.

Female nurses served in Casualty Clearing Stations which were usually housed in tents a relatively safe distance from the Front. In July 1917, three Clearing Stations were set up to cope with casualties from the planned Third Battle of Ypres. Nellie was stationed with the 44th Casualty Clearing Station of the QAIMNS in Brandhoek, near Ypres, near a railway line and a munitions storage area.

On the morning of 21st August 1917, the Germans began shelling the area in order to try to destroy the railway line around Ypres. Two shells narrowly missed the nurses' quarters and another landed on the tent where Nellie, who had been on duty all night, was resting and she was mortally wounded.

Nellie was buried with full military honours in the Military Cemetery at Lijssenthoek, Belgium near Poperinge. Her funeral was attended by four generals, the Surgeon General of the British army and hundreds of officers and other ranks.

She has now been immortalised in this wonderful painting by Søren Hawkes (see below).

Søren Hawkes MA is a British artist living in Ypres, Belgium. His great grandfather served with the Lancashire Fusiliers in WW1 and saw action at The Somme and Passchendaele. His Great Uncle, who was killed in action on 20th February 1915, is listed on Panel 37 of The Menin Gate.

You can see more of Søren's First World War paintings and drawings at passchendaeleprints.com

OLIVE KELSO KING
Australian Ambulance Driver
(1885 – 1958)

Olive May Kelso King was born in Sydney, Australia on 29th June 1885 - she was the daughter of Sir Kelso King, a Sydney-based company director. Olive attended the Sydney Church of England Girls Grammar School and then went to Germany to finish her studies.

She was an adventurer and a keen mountain climber. With companions, Olive climbed Mount Popocatapepl in Mexico.

Olive was on a visit to England when WW1 broke out and immediately purchased a lorry and had it converted it into a 16-seater Ambulance which she drove in France. Olive gave her vehicle the name "Ella the Elephant". In 1915, she joined the Scottish Women's Hospital which had been started by Elsie Inglis the Scottish woman doctor. Olive was sent to a field hospital in Troyes, near Rheims in France.

In November 1915, Olive's unit was despatched to the Eastern Front in Macedonia, where she went to Gevgelija on the border between Greece and Serbia.

Their role in the Balkans was to provide medical assistance to the Serbs in their fight against the Austro-Hungarians, Germans and Bulgarians. King quickly picked up the Serbian language and proved herself brave in the face of Bulgarian fire.

During the Serbian Army retreat from Gevgelija, the hospital had to be evacuated and the 30 women volunteers were aided in the task by 40 Royal Engineers. In a hair-raising escape, the last to leave were Olive and two other women volunteer drivers.

At Olive's suggestion they headed for the railway station and managed to get themselves and their ambulance on to the last train before the station was bombed. In the same retreat, thirteen French ambulance drivers tried to escape by driving out but were captured or killed.

The allies retreated to Salonika, where the SWH established a tent hospital. King remained here for the next two and a half years, even after the SWH had left the country. She resigned from this organisation in mid 1916 and enlisted in the Serbian Army as a driver for the Medical Service at Salonika.

She was attached to the Headquarters of the Medical Service and eventually rose to the rank of sergeant.

She had managed to retain "Ella", despite its broken springs and mechanical problems (many of which she repaired herself) and it was one of only three ambulances available to the Medical Headquarters unit, thus earning the number plate C3. Towards the end of 1916, Olive King contracted malaria and one of her most frequent visitors was Captain Milan "Yovi" Yovitchitch, the Serbian Liaison Officer with the British Army in Salonika. They fell in love and saw each other every day until October 1917, when he was posted to London.

She frequently travelled to the front, transporting men and recovering wounded. Her tireless efforts in evacuating civilians and medical stores driving continuously for 24 hours without a break during the burning of the mainly wooden town of Salonika in August 1917 earned her the Serbian Silver Medal for Bravery.

In 1918 her committed work for the Serbians earned her the Gold Medal for Zealous Conduct.

Before the war's end, supported by over £10,000 raised by her father in Sydney, Olive had established a string of Australian Serbian Canteens to help displaced Serbian families and soldiers. For this work King Alexander of Serbia presented her with the Samaritan Cross and the Cross of the Order of St Sava.

When she returned to Australia, Olive gave lecturers about her war-time experiences and joined the Girl Guide Movement. Olive moved to Melbourne in 1956 where she died on 1st November 1958.

Olive May (Kelso) King standing beside the Alda Motor Ambulance which she supplied and drove for the Scottish Women's Hospitals 1915-1916.

Olive's war medals – from left to right: 1914/15 Star, British War Medal, Victory Medal, Edward VII Coronation, Cross of the Order of St Sava (Serbia), Silver Medal for Bravery Serbia), Gold Medal for Zealous Conduct

MAIRI CHISHOLM
Scottish Motorcyclist & Adventurer
(1896 – 1961)

Mairi *(left in photo above)* was born Mairi Lambert Gooden-Chisholm of Chisholm on 26th February 1896 in Nairn, Scotland. Her parents were Captain Roderick Gooden-Chisholm and his wife Margaret, nee Fraser. Mairi's family were very wealthy and owned a plantation in Trinidad, West Indies.

The family moved to Dorset when Mairi was small and her brother, Uailean was a motorcycle enthusiast who owned a Royal Enfield 425cc motorcycle and used to compete in rallies and at speed trials in Hampshire. When Mairi was eighteen, her father bought her a Douglas motorbike and she used to spend her spare time working on her and her brother's bikes.

It was around that time that Mairi met Elsie Knocker a thirty-year-old widow with a young son. They soon became friends and began to compete in motorcycle rallies.

At Elsie's suggestion the girls volunteered to become dispatch riders for the Women's Emergency Corps in London which was set up to help the war effort and Mairi rode her bike from Dorset to join up. Dr. Hector Monro saw Mairi and recruited her for his Flying Ambulance Corps, an emergency ambulance unit that he proposed to take to Belgium to help wounded soldiers. May Sinclair, the British writer and poet, who contributed financially to the venture, travelled with them to Flanders in September 1914. You can read more about their service in Flanders later...

In 1916, Mairi became engaged to Jack Petrie, a pilot with the British Royal Naval Air Service but he was killed in 1917. In 1918, Elsie and Mairi were gassed and returned to the UK for treatment after which they joined the Women's Auxiliary Air Force, helping to recruit women into the service. Both women received the British Military Medal and were made officers of the Most Venerable Order of the Hospital of St. John of Jerusalem for their extreme bravery in effecting battlefield and No Man's Land rescues and treating the sick and wounded during WW1.

In 1918, Mairi became engaged to 2nd Lt. William Thomas James Hull, of the Royal Flying Corps but their engagement was later called off.

After the war, Mairi discovered that her friend Elsie had not been widowed but was divorced and her strict upbringing meant that she felt she could no longer have any contact with Elsie.

Mairi took up motor racing in spite of bad health due to the gas poisoning during the war. She went back to live in Nairn in Scotland and became a poultry breeder with her childhood friend May Davidson on the Davidson estate. During the 1930s they transferred their business to the island of Jersey where Mairi died on 22nd August 1981. Mairi was also awarded the Military Medal, the Knights Cross of the Order of Leopold II with Palm, the Order of Queen Elisabeth of Belgium and the 1914 Star.

Elsie (right in photo) with Mairi Chisolm displaying their Belgian decorations
(Photo courtesy of National Library of Scotland)

ELSIE KNOCKER
English Nurse & Motorcycle Enthusiast
(1884 – 1978)

Elsie was born Elizabeth Blackall Shapter on 29th July 1884 in Exeter in Devon. She was the youngest child born to Dr. Thomas Lewis Shapter and his wife Charlotte whose maiden name was Bayly. Charlotte died when Elsie was four and Thomas died two years after that. Elsie was adopted by Lewis Edward Upcott - who taught at Marlborough College – and his wife Emily Upcott.

Elsie was educated at St. Nicholas's School in Folkestone and was later sent to a finishing school in Switzerland called Chateau Lutry. She trained as a nurse at the Children's Hip Hospital in Sevenoaks, Kent and married Leslie Duke Knocker in 1906. The couple had a son, Kenneth Duke but the marriage was not a success and they were divorced, after which Elsie went to train as a midwife at Queen Charlotte's Hospital in London. In those days divorce was very much 'frowned upon' so Elsie pretended that her husband had died in Java and that she was a widow.

Elsie's hobby was motorcycling. She joined the Gypsy Motorcycle Club, owned a Scott, a Douglas solo and a Chater-Lea which had a sidecar and soon earned the nickname "Gypsy" as she flew about the Hampshire and Dorset countryside in her dark green leather skirt and coat.

Elsie met Mairi Chisholm through her love of motorcycling and when war broke out in 1914, the pair went up to London to become dispatch riders for the Women's Emergency Corps which had just been formed. Elsie, who as well as being a highly trained nurse was also a mechanic and driver, and Mairi joined Dr. Hector Monro's Flying Ambulance Corps and travelled to Ostend on 25th September 1914, where they nursed the sick and wounded. British poet May Sinclair, who gave financial support to the venture, went as Dr Monro's secretary. May described Elsie as having "an irresistible inclination towards the greatest possible danger".

In January 1916, Elsie married a Belgian Flying Corps pilot called Baron Harold de T'Serclaes but after the ceremony and 'a lightening honeymoon' they both went back to their wartime duties - Elsie to nursing and raising funds for their first-aid station in Pervyse.

In 1918, Elsie and Mairi were gassed and returned to the UK for treatment after which they joined the Women's Auxiliary Air Force, helping to recruit women into the service. Both women received the British Military Medal and were made officers of the Most Venerable Order of the Hospital of St. John of Jerusalem for their extreme bravery in effecting battlefield and No Man's Land rescues and treating the sick and wounded during WW1.

Elsie's second marriage failed when the truth about her first divorce came out and Mairi also abandoned her friend, with whom she had gone through so much, when she found out.

In 1939 when WW2 broke out, Elsie joined the Women's Auxiliary Air Force working with RAF Fighter Command. Her son Wing Commander Kenneth Duke Knocker, was killed on 3rd July 1942 when his plane was shot down over Groningen. Elsie retired in 1942 in order to look after her foster father.

Elsie continued to raise funds for the RAF Association and their Benevolent Fund after WW2 when she lived in the Earl Haig Homes in Ashtead, Surrey. She died on 26th April 1978.

Elsie was also awarded the Military Medal and the Knights Cross of the Order of Leopold II with Palm.

ELSIE & MAIRI IN FLANDERS

Elsie Knocker and Mairi Gooden-Chisholm were two motorbike mad women who met before the First World War competing in motorbike and sidecar trials in Hampshire and Dorset. Mairi was eighteen and Elsie was thirty, divorced and with a young son.

They went up to London on 4th August 1914 when war was declared along with thousands of women all determined to help and ended up in the HQ of the Women's Emergency Corps, formed in 1914 by Evelina Haverfield and Decima Moore with the help of the Women's Social and Political Union to provide women workers to assist with the war effort. The Corps later became the Women's Volunteer Reserve (WVR).

Elsie and Mairi were soon given jobs as dispatch riders and Dr Hector Monro was so impressed with the way Mairi rode her bike that he asked her to join the Flying Ambulance Corps unit that he was putting together to take to Belgium to help the wounded Belgian soldiers. Mairi accepted at once and suggested he talk to Elsie who was a trained nurse.

Munro also took Lady Dorothy Fielding, who spoke French, May Sinclair, the writer and poet who was a generous donor to Monro's causes and Helen Gleason an American whose husband was a journalist covering the Western Front for British and American newspapers.

Doctors, drivers, cooks and medical orderlies were recruited along with two London bus drivers as chauffeurs and with a Daimler and a Fiat, Monro's Flying Ambulance Corps left for Belgium on 25th September 1914, arriving in Ostend on the Princess Clementine.

Elsie and Mairi were initially based in Ghent and soon had their hands full helping Belgian refugees as well as wounded soldiers. Monro's Corps received no official funding from either the French British or Belgian authorities, so May Sinclair's financial aid and the articles she wrote about their work proved invaluable.

All the members of the Corps paid their way with Mairi selling her motorbike in England to fund her trip.

In 1915, Elsie and Mairi split from Dr Munro's Corps and carried on their work in Belgium on their own after a fund-raising journey to England where they collected money and three cars, one of which was a 16 horse power Wolseley ambulance presented to the St. John Ambulance Brigade by the people of Sutton Coldfield.

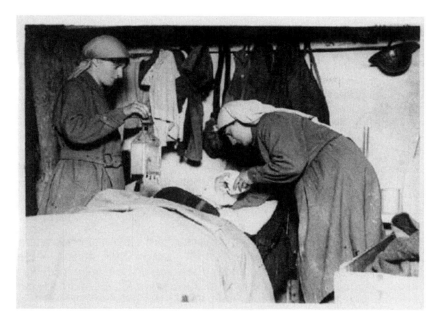

The girls moved to a cottage near Pervyse, where they had previously been based but as the war progressed they had to move to Steenkerke where the Belgian authorities supplied them with food for the wounded soldiers.

As well as their nursing work, they continued raising funds and obtaining food and supplies for themselves and their charges. A generous benefactor arranged for a Harrods hamper to be sent to them via Dunkerque every week and also sent them a Douglas motorbike.

By September 1915, Elsie and Mairi were back in Pervyse, installed in the cellar of a bombed out house.

Among their many adventures, Elsie met Baron Harold de T'Serclaes, a handsome Belgian aviator.

In spite of the war, Elsie and 'Harry' were married on 16th January 1916 after which Elsie was to live in La Panne, where Prince Alexander of Teck was in charge of the British Mission. Mairi wrote to ask her father to join her to help run the medical post.

Elsie and Harry's wedding was a very glamorous affair, in spite of being described as a "Trench marriage" by Tatler magazine, with King Albert and Queen Elizabeth of the Belgians, Prince Alexander of Teck, the Russian military attaché and top brass from the Belgian forces attending the reception.

After a brief honeymoon in England, when Mairi went to collect her father and raise much needed funds, the girls returned to Pervyse. They treated all sorts of ailments as well as tending to wounded soldiers and also set up a recreation tent where the soldiers could relax when not in the trenches. In July 1916, they organized an English sports day with a sack race, three-legged race, tug of war, musical chairs and a hundred-metre race.

Mairi's father left the unit after nine months and Elsie and Mairi again undertook a fund-raising tour of the UK, telling their stories to the British national daily papers and posing for photographs with the medals awarded them by the King of the Belgians. Geraldine Edith Mitton, a British writer, wrote a book about the girls' exploits – "The Cellar-House of Pervyse: A Tale of Uncommon Things from the Journals and Letters of the Baroness T'Serclaes and Mairi Chisholm", which received mixed reviews when it was published but in March 1917 when the girls attended a concert organized to raise funds for them in the Alhambra Theatre in Leicester Square, they received a rapturous welcome.

Mairi too fell in love while in Belgium – with a young British Royal Naval Air Service Officer called Jack Petre from Essex. Sadly, Jack was killed in April 1917.

In early 1918, with the Russians out of the war and the British blockade of German ports beginning to have an effect. Elsie and Mairi went to London to receive another award – The Honorary Associate's Cross of the Order of St. John of Jerusalem.

They attended a concert at the Alhambra in their honour and their photos were in "Tatler" magazine and on show in the British Official War Photographs Exhibition in Grafton Galleries, New Bond Street, London.

On 15th March 1918, Pervyse was bombed constantly and fierce hand to hand fighting took place, as the Germans tried to take Dunkerque which was held by British troops. Elsie and Mairi were right in the middle of the bombing and on 17th March 1918 they were almost killed in an arsenic gas attack during which their terrier dog Shot who had been their constant and faithful companion was killed, though their cats and hens somehow survived. The girls were evacuated to La Panne for treatment in a lorry as their ambulance had been destroyed. From La Panne they went to Lady Hatfield's Hospital in Boulogne, before being sent back to England for treatment.

When they had recovered sufficiently, the girls were recruited by the Women's Royal Air Force to attract volunteers. In July 1918 they were appointed hostel administrators in charge of catering and welfare at Roper Hall, New Eltham, Kent. In September, they went to Hurst Park where they finished the war training women to drive large lorries.

After the war, Elsie and Mairi were demobilised from the Women's Royal Air Force and never saw each other again.

Sources: Wikipedia and
"Elsie and Mairi go to War Two Extraordinary Women on the Western Front" by Diane Atkinson, Preface Publishing, London, 2009

Portrait of Dr Flora Murray by Francis Dodd (1874-1949)
presented to the Royal Free Hospital

Dr FLORA MURRAY
Scottish Doctor
(1869 – 1923)

Flora was born in Cummertrees, Dumfries & Galloway, Scotland in 1869.   She trained at the London School of Medicine for Women and finished her studies in Durham. She worked in Scotland, returning to London in 1905 where she was a Medical Officer at the Belgrave Hospital for Children, then anaesthetist at The Chelsea Hospital for Women.

Flora joined the Women's Social and Political Union in 1908 and was the medical officer to the activists. She spoke at meetings and rallies, joined marches and provided first aid assistance to the suffragettes at demonstrations. She campaigned with other doctors against the forcible feeding of prisoners and treated Emmeline Pankhurst and other hunger-striking suffragettes on their release from prison.

In August 1914, Drs Flora Murray and Elizabeth Garrett Anderson founded the Women's Hospital Corps with the aim of helping wounded soldiers. The British Army were initially sceptical about women treating wounded men, so Dr Murray offered their services to the French Red Cross who asked them to organise a military hospital in Claridges Hotel in Paris. This opened its doors in September 1915.

Sylvia Pankhurst recalled visiting the Claridge's Hotel hospital in Paris in December 1914:

"...we saw her seated far away and small, writing under a shaded lamp. She did not see us till we were close to her; and then she was so much the pitiful, small-voiced woman who had come to my bed-side in those days of the Cat and Mouse Act* that at first I did not notice she was in khaki, a dull, subdued tone of it, with a narrow, dark red piping: the uniform she had chosen for 'the women's hospital corps'...

With her excessive quietude and gentleness, she had overborne many a seemingly cast-iron Army tradition. In defiance of all precedent, she gave equal treatment to officers and privates, placing them side by side in the same wards. ... There was an atmosphere of friendliness and peace..." ("Women's Writing on the First World War", pp 54 – 55 from "The Home Front" by Sylvia Pankhurst).

As the war progressed and the number of casualties grew, the British authorities began to view women doctors in a different light. In 1915, British wounded began to be taken back to England after initial treatment, so the Women's Hospital Corps closed down their operations in France and opened a military hospital in Endell Street in London in what was previously St. Giles Workhouse. Endell Street Hospital, which had 520 beds, was staffed entirely by women.

Flora never married. She died in 1923 and is buried at The Holy Trinity Church with her friend and colleague Dr.Louisa Garrett Anderson near their home in Penn, Buckinghamshire.

*The Cat and Mouse Act was the name given to the Prisoners, Temporary Discharge for Health Act which was introduced in 1913 and designed to weaken the Suffragettes. A suffragette would be arrested and imprisoned. She would go on hunger strike and the authorities would wait until she was too weak to participate in a demonstration when she would be released on licence. If she committed an offence while she was out on licence, a woman would be re-arrested at once and sent back to prison.

Apparently, the tactic was not very successful and added to the strength of the Suffragette's arguments.

The 1918 Representation of the People Act gave women who owned property over the age of thirty the right to vote. It was a start.

Sources: Wikipedia and Cardinal, Agnes, Goldman, Dorothy and Hattaway, Judith, Eds.- "Women's Writing on the First World War" (Oxford University Press, Oxford, 1999). / www.historylearningsite.co.uk/cat_and_mouse_act.htm

Louisa Garret Anderson and Flora Murray

MILLICENT SUTHERLAND

Scottish Founder Of WW1 Ambulances & Hospitals
(1867-1955)

Millicent was born on 20th October 1867 in Fife – the eldest daughter of Robert St. Clair-Erskine, Fourth Earl of Rosslyn and Blanche Adeliza Fitzroy, widow of the Hon. Charles Maynard.

On her 17th birthday (20th October 1884), Millicent married Lord Cromartie Sutherland-Leveson-Gower, Marquess of Stafford, the heir of the third Duke of Sutherland, a title which he inherited – along with the Trentham Hall Estate - on the death of his Father in 1892.

Millicent became a society hostess in London but also showed interest in the welfare of the pottery workers in Staffordshire. In 1900, she founded what would later become the "Duchess Of Sutherland Cripples Guild" which was charity to provide for child workers who had been injured in the potteries. Metalwork items were produced by the Guild and sold in a London showroom to raise funds and Millicent also compiled a book of poetry in 1904 to sell for the charity.

After the death of the Duke in 1913, Millicent married Major Desmond Percy Fitzgerald of the 11th Hussars in October 1914. At the outbreak of War, she funded and set up a Red Cross ambulance unit in France at the age of 46. Millicent was captured by the Germans in 1914 but escaped to Calais, where she managed the British Red Cross Hospital.

The French painter Victor Tardieu (1870 – 1937) who volunteered for the French Army in 1914, painted scenes of the hospital Millicent directed in the summer of 1915. These beautiful paintings have recently (March 2013) been purchased by the Florence Nightingale Museum.

Millicent moved to Roubaix in June 1918 with her Red Cross Unit. For her services during the First World War, Millicent was awarded the French Croix de Guerre, the Belgian Royal Red Cross and the British Red Cross Medal.

After the War, Millicent lived in France and was again captured in 1940. She escaped via Spain and Portugal and went to live in the United States of America, returning to Paris in 1945. She went to live in Orriule in South West France where she died in 1955.

Above:
No 2 of a series of 10 oil paintings by Victor Tardieu (1870-1937) entitled "The Camp In The Oat Field" and painted at Bourbourg during the Summer of 1915. This painting carries the dedication: " à Madame la Duchesse de Sutherland / Hommage respectueux et tres reconaissant d'un simple soldat."
More information and the rest of the paintings can be found at:
www.milicentsutherlandambulance.com

Left: A WW1 postcard entitled "Duchess and Red Cross Nurses"
featuring Millicent Sutherland (far right). These were sold to help raise funds for her Calais war hospital

ELSIE JANIS
American Film Star & Entertainer
(1889 – 1956)

A poet, writer, scriptwriter, lyricist, composer, actress, film star and film director and producer, Elsie was born Elsie Bierbower on 16th March 1889 in Marion County, Ohio. Elsie began her stage career at the age of two, when she was known as "Babie Elsie". Encouraged by her Mother, Jennie, by the age of eleven Elsie was starring in shows and using the name "Little Elsie".

Elsie appeared in several shows on Broadway and in London and was praised by both American and British theatre critics. As her career progressed, Elsie began to act, write scripts and compose music. She raised funds for Liberty Bonds and was very supportive of the War.

She made her London debut in 1914 in "The Passing Show" and won over English audiences as the first shots were fired in World War I. Queen Alexandra attended a performance of one of her plays in 1915 and asked for a photograph, which Elsie sent, along with a copy of one of her poems.

Elise was deeply stirred by the war. Her fiancé, British actor Basil Hallam, was killed in the first months of the conflict when he jumped from an observation balloon and his parachute failed to open. By all accounts Basil was very famous indeed in the pre WW1 period. His death was reported in American newspapers and magazines. They had set up home together in Liverpool after starring together in "The Passing Show" at the Palace Theatre, London in 1914. There's a song which Hallam recorded in June 1914 - "Gilbert the Filbert". It was said that Elsie never got over his death.

After the U.S. entered the war, Elsie and her mother went to France to entertain the troops stationed near the front lines and was thus one of the first American artists to do this in a war fought in a foreign country. They travelled in a chauffeur-driven Cadillac. Some of the camps had a stage ready for Elsie to entertain thousands of soldiers, whereas others had no performance facilities, so Elsie would climb onto the roof of her car to sing, dance and tell jokes.

After the war, Elsie returned to France where she appeared in a show called "Elsie Janis and her Gang in a Bomb-Proof Review" – 1919 – 1920 with a cast consisting of former soldiers, nurses and other WW1 workers. Elsie wrote and published several books and anthologies of poetry, among them a book about her WW1 experiences - "The Big Show: My Six Months with the American Expeditionary Forces" (1919) which she later recreated in a show called "Behind the Lines" (1926).

In 1932, Elsie married Gilbert Wilson and they lived in Sleepy Hollow, New York. Elsie continued to act, sing, write, appear in films, produce, direct and compose and later moved to Hollywood where she lived until she died in February 1956 with her friend Mary Pickford at her side. She left most of her estate to her housekeeper – Ellen Lamb – and to her chauffeur – Frank Reme – who had been with Elsie since driving her to entertain the American troops of the Western Front in The First World War.

She made her last film in 1940 with Wendy Barrie and Peter Cushing called 'Women in War.'

Elsie has a star on the Hollywood Walk of Fame for her contribution to the motion picture industry.

Photos:
Above: Elsie Janis' star on Hollywood's Walk Of Fame

Next Page

Top: Sheet music for a popular song by Elsie and Basil Hallam from their hit West End show "The Passing Show"

Bottom: Elsie entertaining US troops in France on a makeshift stage

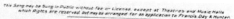

YOU'RE HERE AND I'M HERE.

WORDS BY
HARRY B. SMITH.

MUSIC BY
JEROME D. KERN.

SUNG BY
Miss Elsie Janis & Basil Hallam

IN
ALFRED BUTT'S
Successful Production

THE
PASSING
SHOW.

(PALACE THEATRE, LONDON.)

Book and Lyrics by
Arthur Wimperis.

MUSIC COMPOSED AND ARRANGED
BY
HERMAN
FINCK.

PHOTO BY FOULSHAM & BANFIELD.

COPYRIGHT.

Price 2/-

LONDON:
FRANCIS, DAY & HUNTER,
138-140, CHARING CROSS ROAD, W.C.

NEW YORK:
T.B.HARMS & FRANCIS, DAY & HUNTER INC, 62-64, WEST 45TH STREET.

Copyright MCMXIV in all Countries by T.B.Harms & Francis, Day & Hunter.

GERTRUDE BELL

English Writer, Traveller & Archaeologist
(1868-1926)

Gertrude was born into a wealthy family in County Durham in on 14th July 1868. Her mother died when she was three which meant Gertrude had a close relationship with her father, Sir Hugh Bell, 2nd Baronet, three times Mayor of Middlesborough. When Gertrude was seven, her father married Florence Bell, a playwright and writer of children's fiction.

Gertrude was educated at Queen's College, London and then went to Lady Margaret Hall, Oxford where she obtained a First Class Honours Degree in Modern History. After graduation, Gertrude travelled to Persia with her uncle, Sir Frank Lascelles, who was appointed British Minister at Tehran (similar to the post of Ambassador).

The next few years were spent travelling especially in Arabia, mountaineering and learning languages. Gertrude was fluent in Arabic, Persian, French, German, Italian and Turkish. During her travels in Arabia, Gertrude met T.E. Lawrence, with whom she shared a love of the Arab peoples. Gertrude translated and published the work of the fourteenth century Sufi poet, Hafiz into English to great acclaim.

When war broke out in 1914, Gertrude went to work with the Red Cross in France. In 1915, she was summoned to Cairo to work for the Arab Bureau. On 3rd March 1916 she was sent to Basra and on 10th March 1917 to Baghdad.

According to Gertrude's reports at the time, "…there were not many (if any) permanent solutions for calming the divisive forces at work in that part of the world".

When the Ottoman Empire was split up after the War, Gertrude was given the task of reporting on the situation in Mesopotamia as, by that time, she was an expert on the tribes in the area. As such, she was heavily involved in establishing and administering the modern state of Iraq. .

Gertrude returned to England in 1925 where her family fortunes had suffered in the aftermath of the war. She returned to Baghdad and was treated for Pleurisy. Her brother, Hugo, died of Typhoid.

Gertrude died in Baghdad on 12th July 1926 in what at that time was known as the British Mandate of Mesopotamia and is modern day Iraq.

Her Obituary, published in "The Geographical Journal" and written by a colleague D.G. Hogarth, stated:

"No woman in recent time has combined her qualities – her taste for arduous and dangerous adventure with her scientific interest and knowledge, her competence in archaeology and art, her distinguished literary gift, her sympathy for all sorts and condition of men, her political insight and appreciation of human values, her masculine vigour, hard common sense and practical efficiency – all tempered by feminine charm and a most romantic spirit."

After Gertrude's death, her stepmother, by then Dame Florence Bell, published two volumes of Gertrude's letters written during the preceding twenty years.   Gertrude is buried in the British Cemetery in Baghdad.

A stained glass window in the church of St. Lawrence, East Rounton, North Yorkshire, is dedicated to her memory.

Gertrude Bell's workers at the Byzantine excavation in Binbirkilise, Turkey in 1907.

MARY RITER HAMILTON
Canadian Artist
(1873- 1954)

Mary was a painter and her amazing work painting pictures of the Battlefields of France and Belgium in the immediate aftermath of the First World War, makes an important contribution to the history of the Great War and, as a consequence, Mary really deserves a mention here.

Mary was born on 11th February 1873 in Ontario and was raised in Clearwater, Manitoba, where her family moved when she was small.

Mary married and attended art classes. After the death of her husband, her art teachers, who had all studied in Paris, suggested she go to Europe to complete her studies. She spent eighteen months in Berlin and then moved to Paris for eight years, where several of her paintings were accepted for display in the Salon.

In 1906, Mary went back to Canada to look after her Mother who had been taken ill. In 1907, she returned to Paris and continued painting and exhibiting her work.

In 1911, Mary returned to Canada and nursed her Mother until her death. After her Mother's death, she organized an exhibition, showing over 100 of her paintings. Following the success of her exhibition, Mary painted Canadian scenes to take to Paris for an exhibition of Canadian landscape paintings.

The War in Europe forced her to change her plans and remain in Canada for the duration of World War 1. Mary had hoped to be commissioned as an official War Artist but she was not allowed to do that.

However, at the end of the War, Mary was commissioned by the Amputation Club of British Columbia to produce artwork for their Veterans' Magazine "The Gold Stripe", showing the battlefields as they looked immediately after the War. So she travelled to France in early 1919, staying initially with the Canadian troops based in Arras until they returned home, when she lived among the Chinese workers who were employed to clear away the mess left by the War. She lived in an old army hut.

It is difficult for us to imagine what life was like for Mary in the "no man's land" of the Aftermath of the War – conditions during the War we know were terrible because local drinking water was contaminated early on in the War and supplies of water had to be transported from England and boiled before use.

Mary lived alone and at that time there were roaming gangs of deserters and robbers and, along with serious food shortages, she was in constant personal danger.

Journalists at the time described her exploits thus:

"to go alone into the nightmare country of the Somme after Armageddon had passed - a country peopled by ghosts, where every rustle of a leaf evokes a shudder and the very pools have been poisoned by the abominable breath of war—in order with paint and canvas to produce a lasting vision of the Inferno before kindly Nature had covered up the scars and sores inflicted by the sacrilegious hand of men ..."

"Dauntless Canadian Woman Tells of Grim Experience While Painting the Nightmare Land of the Somme"; "In Vivid Interview, Mary Riter Hamilton Talks of Her Three Years Work Alone in the Heart of Devastated France";

"Menaced by Human Jackals"; "Solitary Artist Was Continually at the Mercy of Prowling Gangs of Criminals"; "Cut-throats of No Man's Land Made One Attempt to Kill Her".

Mary painted 350 paintings in the three years she spent on the Battlefields. All this work took its toll on her health, she became ill and lost an eye. Her work was extensively exhibited in France, including at the Paris Opera House and in England and she was decorated – receiving the highest decoration a woman could receive in France at that time.

When she returned to Canada, she donated all of the paintings to the nation.

Her experiences changed everything, including her approach to her work and Mary decorated textiles for a living when she returned to Canada. She never appeared to receive in Canada the acclaim due to her for her amazing work.

She died in Vancouver, British Columbia on 22nd January 1954. Her work is surely a testament to her talent and her courage.

Mont St Eloi, near Arras
by Mary Riter Hamilton

Interior Of A Ruined Church, Arras
by Mary Riter Hamilton

INEZ MILHOLLAND
Feminist Activist & Journalist
(1886 – 1916)

Inez was born on 6th August 1886 in Brooklyn, New York, into a wealthy family and went on to become a champion of the cause for votes for women. Inez's father, John Elmer Milholland, was initially a reporter with the newspaper The New York Herald Tribune.

After attending finishing schools in London and Berlin, Inez obtained a BA from Vassar College in New York. Her ambition was to study law but she was not able to attend either Oxford or Cambridge because they did not accept female students to study law at that time and instead enrolled at New York University Law School. She was accepted at the Bar in 1912.

Her causes were far reaching: in addition to prison reform, she sought world peace and worked for equality for African Americans.

Milholland was a member of the NAACP, the US Women's Trade Union League, the Equality League of Self Supporting Women in New York (Women's Political Union), the US National Child Labor Committee, and the Fabian Society.

She was also involved in the National American Woman Suffrage Association, which later branched into the grassroots radical National Woman's Party. She became a leader and a popular speaker on the campaign circuit of the NWP, working closely with Alice Paul and Lucy Burns.

In 1913, at the age of 27, Milholland made her most memorable appearance, as she helped organize the suffrage parade in Washington D.C., scheduled to take place the day before President Woodrow Wilson's inauguration. She led the parade wearing a crown and a long white cape while riding a large white horse named "Gray Dawn" (in photo above).

Inez married Eugen Jan Boissevain, a Dutch Importer, in London in July 1913.

At the outbreak of the First World War, Inez went to Italy as war correspondent for a Canadian Newspaper and had access to the front lines in that theatre of the War. Her articles preached pacifism and led to her expulsion from Italy by the Italian Government of the day.

She was also a leading figure on Henry Ford's (of Ford Motor Company fame...) ill-fated Peace Ship expedition of late 1915, steaming across the Atlantic with a team of pacifist campaigners who hoped to give impetus to a negotiated settlement to the First World War. However, she left the ship in Stockholm because the trip was unorganised and dissension had ensued between passengers. Her role was fictionalised by the British novelist Douglas Galbraith in his novel "King Henry".

Milholland vehemently protested against America's involvement in World War I. She was a workers' lawyer and was involved in the production of the socialist journal, "The Masses".

In 1916, she went on a tour in the West - speaking for women's rights as a member of the National Woman's Party – despite suffering from pernicious anaemia and despite the admonitions of her family who were concerned about her deteriorating health. On October 22, 1916, she collapsed in the middle of a speech in Los Angeles, and was rushed to Good Samaritan Hospital. Despite repeated blood transfusions, she died on November 25, 1916.

Milholland's last public words were:

"Mr. President, how long must women wait for liberty"

Her widower, Eugen Jan Boissevain, married Edna St. Vincent Millay in 1923 and Edna wrote this poem as a tribute to Inez. It was read out on 18th November 1923 at the unveiling of a statue of three leaders of the cause for equal rights for women at the Capitol in Washington DC.

"To Inez Milholland"
by Edna St. Vincent Millay

Upon this marble bust that is not I
Lay the round, formal wreath that is not fame;
But in the forum of my silenced cry
Root ye the living tree whose sap is flame.
I, that was proud and valiant, am no more; ---
Save as a dream that wanders wide and late,
Save as a wind that rattles the stout door,
Troubling the ashes in the sheltered grate.
The stone will perish; I shall be twice dust.
Only my standard on a taken hill
Can cheat the mildew and the red-brown rust
And make immortal my adventurous will.
Even now the silk is tugging at the staff:
Take up the song; forget the epitaph.

Edna St. Vincent Millay (1892 – 1950) was an
American lyrical poet, playwright and feminist
activist. She received the Pulitzer Prize for Poetry
in 1923 and was only the third woman to win the
award for poetry

The poem that Edna read is the sonnet was
originally written as "The Pioneer," which
encouraged women to continue to fight for equal
rights.

It is unclear if Edna wrote the lines about Anthony,
Stanton, and Mott (the women's rights pioneers in
the marble statue) or about Inez — or about all of
them. However, by 1928, Edna had retitled the
sonnet "To Inez Milholland."

Edna St Vincent Millay
(Library Of Congress)

MILDRED ALDRIDGE
American Writer
(1853-1928)

Mildred was born in Providence, Rhode Island, USA on 16th November 1853. She grew up and was educated in Boston, became a primary school teacher and then a journalist, writing for the "Boston Home Journal", The Boston Journal" and the "Boston Herald".

Mildred went to live in France in 1898, initially in Paris where she met Gertrude Stein and Alice B. Toklas and worked as a foreign correspondent and translator.

When she was sixty, Mildred decided to retire and looked for a house to buy in the countryside around Paris. In June 1914, she moved to Huiry, where she found a delightful house overlooking the River Marne, which she began to renovate.

The House in Huiry
(Photo taken from A Hilltop On The Marne)

Those of you who know about the First World War will be familiar with the Battle of the Marne and can therefore imagine that Mildred's dream of a peaceful retirement away from the hustle and bustle of the capital was suddenly shattered in August 1914.

Mildred's accounts of what life was like for a civilian woman in her part of the world during the First World War are fascinating and were published in book form, based on her letters to a friend in the United States of America - "A Hilltop on the Marne" in 1915, "On the Edge of the War Zone" in 1917, "The Peak of the Load" in 1918 and "When Johnny comes Marching Home" in 1919.

Mildred also wrote a novel about her experiences – "Told in a French Garden, August 1914" which was published in 1916. She also wrote her auto-biography, which she called "Confessions of a Breadwinner" which was never published but is stored away in the Schlesinger Library at Harvard University.

In 1922, Mildred was awarded the Legion of Honour, for it was widely felt that her books, which were very successful in America, had contributed to America joining the war.

Mildred died on 19th February 1928 and is buried in the churchyard of the Church of St. Denis in Quinchy-Voisons.

I first became aware of Mildred Aldrich through looking at Matt Jacobsen's wonderful website OldMagazineArticles.com

Now, I am 'haunted' by Mildred Aldrich's "Hilltop on the Marne" - it spans about two months from July to September 1914 and is in the form of extracts from letters written to a friend in America. It is, to my mind, extremely well written and makes you want to find out what happened next.

THE ROAD TO THE MARNE
Taken from the point where the author stopped with the captain of the bicycle corps

Mildred travelled to Paris and back twice during those early days of WW1 and, in spite of earnest requests from departing neighbours that she should accompany them, she refused to leave her new home. One of the first things that happened was that a man with a drum marched through the streets of the village telling everyone about general mobilisation. It is hard for us to imagine those days when there was no radio or television and few people had telephones, let alone mobile phones, computers and the Internet.

Mildred described being relieved that she stayed put when she heard reports of how the refugees were stuck on the roads. She also described the arrival of various groups of soldiers - two lots of British and one of French - and her efforts to help them with refreshments. When the French arrived, some were billeted in her house.

I wanted to know what happened to the Uhlans who were rumoured to be camped out in a wood near the River, and the fate of the gallant Captain S- of The King's Own Yorkshire Light Infantry, 13th Infantry Brigade, 15th Division of the British Expeditionary Force, one of the first British soldiers Mildred came into contact with when she offered refreshments to his tired troops. Captain S- returned several times while in the area to make sure Mildred was all right.

Another soldier who asked Mildred for help was Lt. Edwin Allan James Edwards from Brixton, London who needed somewhere for his troops to wash and rest. Lt. Edwards was wounded on 15th October 1914, leading his men into battle at Givenchy. He was sent back to England where he died in the Fishmongers Hall Hospital, London Bridge on 31st December 1914. He is buried in St Mary's Churchyard at Long Ditton, Surrey.

Facebook Group WW1 Buffs informed me that The Western Front Association Thames Valley Branch published details in their September 2011 Newsletter of the "Captain S" mentioned in Mildred Aldrich's "Hilltop on the Marne", including photographs. Captain S- was John Edmund Simpson from London. He was killed at Messines on 31st October 1914 and is commemorated on the Menin Gate Memorial at Ypres, Belgium.

Mildred and a friend visited the graves of many of the soldiers killed in the early days of the war. They travelled on 5th December 1914 by car, following the line of the fighting on 6th and 7th September 1914. Pilgrimages to the cemeteries had begun on All Souls Day – 2nd November – 1914 but Mildred preferred to wait and go when the crowds had thinned out.

Photo: German Uhlans - courtesy of WW1 Buffs Facebook Page.

FLORA SANDES
English Aid Worker & Serbian Army Soldier
(1876 – 1956)

Flora was the daughter of Samuel Sandes, Rector of Whitchurch, County Cork and Sophia Julia (née Bresnard). She was born on 22nd January 1876 in Yorkshire but the family moved to East Anglia when Flora was nine years old. Flora was educated at home by a governess. She was a tomboy and learnt to drive, driving an old French sports car.

She worked as a Secretary but in her spare time she trained with the Female Nursing Yeomanry, studying First Aid. When WW1 broke out, Flora volunteered to nurse but was turned down because she was not qualified.

However, she joined a St. Johns Ambulance unit raised by American archaelogist Mabel Grouitch (nee Dunlap), who had met and married a Serbian during a dig in Greece and organised a group of British women to travel to Serbia in August 1914 to help with the situation on the Eastern Front.

There, Flora joined the Serbian Red Cross and was assigned to an ambulance with a unit of the Second Infantry Regiment of the Serbian Army. Flora became separated from her nursing unit as the Serbian Army retreated from Albania and for safety enrolled in the Serbian Army as an ordinary soldier.

She was the only British woman to do this. She was soon promoted to the rank of Corporal and fought bravely. She was wounded during the Serbian advance on Bitola. For her bravery, Flora was awarded the Order of the Karadorde's Star and promoted to Sergeant Major.

Due to her injuries, Flora was unable to continue fighting and instead ran a hospital. At the end of the War, she became an officer.

Flora married a fellow officer and remained in Serbia. During the Second World War she was briefly interned by the Germans.

After the death of her husband, Flora returned to live in England, where she died on 25th November 1956 in Suffolk. Her story can be read in a recently published book by Louise Miller entitled "A Fine Brother: The Life of Flora Sandes", published by Alma Books.

ECATERINA TEODOROIU
Rumanian Soldier
(1894-1917)

Ecaterina Teodoroiu was born in Oltenia, Rumania on 15th January 1894a nd was about to become a teacher when Romania joined the war. She joined the Rumanian Army in October 1916, first working as a nurse but, after her brother Nicolae, a Sergeant in the army, was killed, she decided to fight.

She was taken prisoner but managed to escape, killing several German soldiers. Wounded in November 1916, she returned and was promoted to Second Lieutenant in command of 25 men.

Her bravery in action earned her the Military Virtue Medal 1st Class but she was killed at the Battle of Maraseti on 3rd September 1917, where she was hit in the chest by German machine gun fire. According to some accounts, her last words before dying were: "Forward, men, I'm still with you!"

Ectaterina became the first female Rumanian war hero to be honoured with a statue – designed by Dumitru Mataoanu and unveiled in 1925 in Slatina (photo left). Numerous other monuments have been built to her over the years

A film about her life was made in 1978.

MILUNKA SAVIC
Serbian Army Soldier
(1888- 1973)

Milunka Savic was born in Born 1888, Koprivnica, Serbia in 1888. When her brother was served with his call-up papers for the Second Balkan War in 1913, Milunka elected to take his place.   She cut her hair, wore men's clothes and fought bravely, receiving a medal and promotion for her bravery.   She was wounded and only then was her subterfuge discovered.

In 1914, in the early days of World War I, Savić was awarded her first Karađorđe Star with Swords after the Battle of Kolubara. She received her second Karađorđe Star (with Swords) after the Battle of Crna Reka in 1916 when she captured 23 Bulgarian soldiers single-handedly.

During the war, she was awarded the French Légion d'Honneur (Legion of Honour) twice, Croix De Guerre with Gold Palm, Russian Cross of St. George, British medal of the Most Distinguished Order of St Michael and the Serbian Miloš Obilić medal.

After the war, Milunka turned down an offer to go and live in France and receive a French pension in recognition of her contribution. However, in the interwar period, she was more or less ignored in the new Yugoslavia and had to take menial jobs.

During the German occupation of Yugoslavia in World War II, Milunka refused to attend a banquet organised by Milan Nedić, which was to be attended by German generals and officers. She was arrested and taken to Banjica concentration camp, where she was imprisoned for ten months.

After the advent of socialism in 1945, she was given a state pension, and continued to live in her house in Belgrade's Voždovac neighbourhood.

By the late 1950s her daughter was in hospital, and she was living in a crumbling house in Voždovac with her three adopted children: Milka, a forgotten child from the railway station in Stalac; Radmila-Višnja; and Zorka, a fatherless girl from Dalmatia.

Later, when she attended the jubilee celebrations wearing her military medals, other military officers spoke with her and heard of her courageous actions. News spread and she finally gained recognition for her achievements. In 1972, public pressure and a newspaper article highlighting her difficult housing and financial situation led to her being given a small apartment by the Belgrade City Assembly.

She died in 1973 and there is a street in Belgrade named after her.

WOMEN PILOTS

A lot of people seem to be surprised when we mention bombing raids and women pilots during the First World War, however there were indeed both. Balloons had been used in combat since the French Revolution. Artillery batteries had become used to firing in the air during the Franco-Prussian War. Italy used planes in Libya from 1910 – 1911 and in The Balkans 1912 – 1913.

Air travel was taking off during the years before the First World War – there were flying clubs in towns all over Britain and experiments were made with local flights. Charles Rolls of Rolls Royce fame, achieved a non-stop double flight crossing the English Channel and back on 2nd June 1910.

The first woman to fly across the English Channel was an American - Harriet Quimby (photo above) - who made the flight in 59 minutes, taking off from Dover on 16th April 1912. Harriet was killed in a flying accident on 1st July 1912.

Other notable American women pilots of this period include Katherine Wright (sister of the Wright Brothers) who flew in 1909, Baronesse Bessica Raiche – 1910, Blanche Stuart Scott, Matilde Moissant, Katherine and Marjorie Stinson and Ruth Law who took part in fund-raising activities.

Hélène DUTRIEU (1877 – 1961), BELGIAN, was a truly Inspirational Woman – she is described as having been a cycling world champion, stunt cyclist, stunt motorcyclist, racing car driver, stunt driver, pioneer aviator, wartime ambulance driver and director of a military hospital.

Hélène was born in Tournai in Belgium on 10th July 1877. Her Father was an Army officer. She left school at 14 to go out to work. She became a track cyclist and in 1895 won the women's world record for distance cycled in an hour.

In 1908 Hélène was invited to pilot a Santos-Dumont monoplane. She crashed on take off, wrecking the plane.

On 19th April 1910, she was the first woman pilot to fly with a passenger. The same year, she flew from Ostend to Bruges in Belgium.

During the First World War, Hélène drove ambulances and later became the director of a military hospital at Val-de-Grace. She was sent to the USA in 1915 by the French Red Cross on a lecture tour for propaganda purposes.

In 1956 she created the Hélène Dutrieu-Mortier Cup with a prize for the French or Belgian woman pilot who made the longest non-stop flight each year. She died in Paris on 26th June 1961.

Dutrieu the cycling champion

There were also some fascinating **Russian** women pilots who came to prominence prior to and during World War One.

Princess Eugenie M. Shakhovskaya (photo left) was Russia's first woman military pilot.

She received her pilot's licence in 1911 and tried unsuccessfully to join the Italian Air Service during the 1912 Tripolitanian War.

At the start of the First World War, she wrote directly to the Czar for permission to serve in the Imperial Russian Air Service as a military pilot. The Czar was impressed and she was enrolled as an Ensign of Engineers.

In November 1914, she was sent to the First Field Air Squadron on the Russian North Western Front. However, instead of being allowed to fly, Eugenie was repeatedly sexually assaulted by the officers. When she tried to escape to enemy lines, she was arrested for treason and sentenced to death by firing squad.

The Tsar commuted her sentence to life imprisonment in a convent because she was pregnant.

During the Russian Revolution, Eugenie became a Communist and worked for the "Cheka" secret police as an executioner. She became addicted to drugs and was killed by one of her colleagues after she shot and killed her own assistant for no apparent reason while under the influence of drugs.

Shakhovskaya and Abramovich Vsevolod Mikhaylovich in 1913

Helen Samsonova received her pilot's licence in 1913 at the Imperial Moscow Aviation Association Flying School. In the First World War, she served as a nurse then a chauffeur and finally managed to get a situation in flying with the Fifth Army Corps Air Squadron as a reconnaissance pilot.

She was involved in an incident with a fellow male officer where she fired a pistol and was transferred out of the Squadron due to "emotional temperament". In the Russian Civil War, Helen served as an observer on reconnaissance and artillery missions. Samsanova died in 1958 at the age of 68.

Lyubov Golanchikova (above) was a popular stage actress with the stage name Milly Moore. She received her pilot's certificate at the Gatchina Military Flying School in 1911.

In November 1912, while flying with Anthony Fokker's company in Germany, she set a women's altitude record of 7218 feet in a Fokker Eindecker. Golanchikova became an overnight sensation and the German army adopted the Fokker as their military aircraft of choice.

She was a test pilot for the Russians in the early part of the First World War and then returned to the stage.

She returned to flying during the Russian Civil War and joined the Training Squadron of the Red Air Fleet. She flew several sorties for the Reds and spent much time training new Red pilots. For some reason, she fled to Germany after the civil war and eventually emigrated to the USA. She ended up driving a taxi cab in New York, where she died in 1961 at the age of 72.

Princess Sophie Alexandrovna Dolgorunaya (photo above)
obtained her pilot's licence in 1914. She volunteered for the air
service in 1917 and flew missions with the 26th Corps Air Squadron
for nine months. Because of her connection to the Imperial family
she was demobilized after the October Revolution. Little else is
known about her.

Nadesha Degtereva (photo above) disguised herself as a boy and used a male friend's medical certificate to enrol for military flight training. She qualified for combat flying and was posted to a reconnaissance unit on the Galician Front.

On one of her missions behind enemy lines in Spring 1915, Nadesha's aircraft was involved in a dog flight. Austrian fighter planes riddled her aircraft with bullets and injured her in the arm and the leg.

She managed to fly her damaged plane back to her own airfield but her real name and gender were discovered when she reached hospital.

The Russian press feted her as a national heroine but the Army was less happy and sent her away to the Caucasus Front.

Elfriede Riote
(Source: The Day Book. (Chicago, Ill.) 1911-1917, August 20, 1914)

ELFRIEDE RIOTE (1879 - 1960) - GERMAN - was the first woman Zeppelin airship pilot. Elfriede was born in Alsace on 12th April 1879, daughter of a senior civil servant. Alsace was German at that time. In April 1914, she took her tests on the Parseval-Luftschiff P VI and in July of that year she gained her pilot's licence.

Elfriede was not allowed to fly airships during the First World War so she concentrated on lecturing about flying. Elfriede moved to Berlin after the War, built a guesthouse on the Island of Ruegen in the Baltic Sea and gave lectures about aviation.

Marie Marvingt
French Pilot
(1875 – 1963)

Marie was born in Aurillac, Cantal. The family moved to Metz which, it should be noted was German at that time, where they lived from 1880 – 1889. After her Mother's death, Marie at the age of fourteen. took charge of the family and they moved to Nancy.

Encouraged by her Father, Marie became an accomplished athlete, winning medals in swimming, fencing, shooting, ski jumping, speed skating, sledging and bobsleighing. She also excelled at water polo, horse riding, athletics, boxing, martial arts, fencing, tennis, golf, hockey, football, mountaineering and circus skills. In 1890, at the age of fifteen, Marie canoed from Nancy to Koblenz in Germany – more than 400 kilometers (250 miles).

In 1901 Marie made her first balloon flight as a passenger and in 1907 she piloted a balloon herself, going solo in September 1909.

She piloted a balloon across the English Channel on 26th October 1909 and, that same year, Marie flew in a plane as a passenger and then studied fixed-wing aviation with Hubert Latham. She was the second woman to be licensed to fly a monoplane.

During the First World War, Marie disguised herself as a man, something that she had to do because woman were not taken seriously when they tried to sign up. Helped by a French Infantry Lieutenant, she served at the Front as a Soldier, 2nd Class in the French 42nd Battalion of Foot Soldiers. She was discovered and sent home.

Air Ambulance Pioneer

Marie was the first woman to fly missions as a bomber pilot. She was also a qualified nurse and worked tirelessly to try to establish a global air ambulance service. In 1915, Marie became the first woman in the world to fly combat missions when she took part in a bombing raid on a German military base in Metz, for which she received the Croix de Guerre.

Marie's efforts would appear to have begun to bear fruit for, in 1915, during the retreat of the French Army from Serbia a group of wounded men were saved from capture by being flown out on combat aircraft.

This is commonly accepted as the first recorded case of an aircraft being used as an air ambulance to evacuate an injured man.

For the remainder of the war, Marie served as a Red Cross nurse and between the wars, she travelled extensively lecturing about the concept of 'aeromedical evacuation'.

On her 80th birthday, Marie was flown over Nancy in an American jet fighter. She began to study the piloting of helicopters but never earned her licence. At the age of 86 she cycled from Nancy to Paris.

Marie died at the age of 88 at Laxou in North-Eastern France.

FEMALE SECRET AGENTS IN WW1

Brussels was occupied by the Germans during the First World War. Although they got within 30 miles of the French Capital City, nevertheless Paris remained free for the duration of WW1, which meant it was a meeting place for all sorts of people.

The popularly accepted idea of a mysterious "Femme Fatale" figure such as **Mata Hari** (photo above) as being a typical spy during the First World War could not be further from the truth. Mata Hari, who lived in Paris, is believed to have been a spy but the singer Mistinguette apparently did more.

In the years prior to the War a parliamentary study revealed that there was 'widespread German infiltration' but 'there was no organisation' of counter-espionage. So the British Government brought the Secret Service Bureau into being. Notable male spies were Sidney Reilly and the writer W. Somerset Maugham.

MARTHE CNOCKAERT
Belgian Spy
(1892 – 1966)

Marthe was born on 28th October 1892 in Westrozebeke in the west of Belgium. When The First World War broke out Marthe was a student at Ghent University and had trained as a nurse.

Her village was burnt by the advancing Germans and Marthe became separated from her family. In 1915, she went to work in a German military hospital in Roulers, Belgium, where her family had found shelter when their home was burnt down.

There, Marthe was recruited into the British Intelligence by a Belgian neighbour, working with two other Belgian women agents. For two years Marthe worked as a nurse in the German hospital and also in her parents' café, gathering vital intelligence information for the British.

A German agent who was billeted in her home tried to recruit Marthe to work for the Germans and she worked for a time as a double agent.

When this became too complicated she arranged for the German agent to be killed. Marthe discovered a disused sewer tunnel system under a German ammunition dump and placed explosives there. Unfortunately, Marthe lost her watch, which was engraved with her initials as she placed the explosives and that led to her capture. Marthe was sentenced to death but due to her expertise as a nurse and the fact that she had been nursing German wounded for which she had received the Iron Cross, the sentence was commuted and Marthe spent two years in prison in Ghent.

After the War, Marthe received recognition for her work from the British and the French. She married a British Army Officer – John McKenna and wrote her memoirs, for which Winston Churchill wrote a foreword, as well as novels. In 1933 a film of Marthe's life story was made called "I was a Spy" with the actress Madeleine Carroll in the starring role. Marthe died in Westrozebeke in 1966.

ELSBETH SCHRAGMüLLER
German Spy
(1887 – 1940)

Born 7th August 1887 in Schlusselburg, Prussia, the eldest of four children. Her Father was a Prussian Army Officer.

Part of Elsbeth's childhood was spent living with her Grandmother in Münster and it was from her Grandmother that Elspeth received her initial education.

She finished her studies at Albert-Ludwigs University in Freiburg and was one of the first German women to be awarded a degree.

Elsbeth moved to Belgium in WW1 where she worked on opening and intercepting letters. She was then transferred to the work of collecting information in Lille and given the code name of "Fraulein Doktor".

A European film called "Fraulein Doktor" and released in 1969 is based on her life. After the War, Elsbeth went to live in Munich where she died in 1940 of bone tuberculosis.

DESPINA STORCH
Turkish Spy
(1895 – 1918)

Despina was born in Istanbul in the Ottoman Empire on 1st January 1895.

When she was 17, Despina married a Frenchman – Paul Storch – but the marriage did not last long.

Despina travelled extensively using false names – in Paris she called herself "Madame Nezie". In London and Madrid, "Mrs Hesketh".

In Rome she was Madame Davidovitch, in New York Madame Despina and in Washington the Baroness de Belville. Despina was very beautiful, spoke fluent French and was a very good dancer so she was in great demand at social events where she mixed with high-ranking military personnel and ambassadors, etc. Despina was accompanied in her travels by a man called Baron Henri de Bellville.

In Madrid the couple were observed meeting German agents so they left there and travelled to Havana. Some time later, in the company of two others – a German lady called Mrs Elizabeth Charlotte Nix and a French Count called Robert de Clairmont – Despina and Baron Henri arrived in New York. The authorities became suspicious and placed them under observation.

When Despina realised what had happened, they tried to obtain French passports and travel to Cuba but they were arrested and sent to Ellis Island for questioning where they all became ill. Despina died of pneumonia on 30th March 1918. The "New York Sun" newspaper described her as "the most romantic spy suspect America has yet known."

MARTHE RICHARD
French Spy
(1889 – 1982)

When she was 14, Marthe went to live in Nancy where she was apprenticed to a tailor.

She became a prostitute in 1905 but was forced to move to Paris when she was accused of giving a client Syphilis.

In Paris, Marthe met and married a rich industrialist called Henri Richer. In 1912, Henri Richer purchased an aeroplane which he piloted himself. Marthe flew the plane herself for the first time in 1913, claiming to have broken the record for the Le Crotoy – Zurich flight. In fact she flew the plane to Burgundy and had it taken by train to a station just outside Zurich then flew the remainder of the journey.

In 1914, Marthe helped to create the Patriotic Union of French Women Pilots and after the death of her husband in 1916, she became an agent working for British Intelligence. She was given the task of spying on the Naval Attaché of the German Navy in Madrid – Von Krohn. When she returned to Paris, she discovered that her handler was a double agent and had him arrested and imprisoned.

After the War, Marthe wrote her memoirs and published them under the title "My life as a spy in the French Service" which was made into a film in 1937. Following the success of her book, Marthe was awarded the French Legion d'honneur. During the 1940s and 50s, Marthe was a prominent campaigner for the rights and welfare of prostitutes in France. She died in 1982, aged 92

SARAH AARONSOHN
(1890 – 1917)

Jewish Spy Who Worked For British Inteligence

Sarah was born and died in Zichron Yaakov in Israel which, at the time of the First World War was under Turkish rule and part of the Ottoman Empire.

Sarah went to live in Istanbul where she was married but returned home when the marriage failed. On the journey home, Sarah saw the results of the Genocide of the Armenian people and was so horrified by what she witnessed that she volunteered to help the British cause, joining Nili, which was a group of Jewish spies working for the British in World War One.

Sarah travelled widely throughout the Ottoman Empire collecting information vital to the British and delivered it to them in Egypt. In September 1917, the Turks caught a carrier pigeon which was taking a message from Sarah to the British so they arrested several people in Zichron Yaakov, tortured and interrogated them. After four days of constant torture, Sarah was concerned she would break so she killed herself with a pistol that had been hidden under a tile in a bathroom and so saved the lives of her colleagues.

She is known as "The Heroine of Mili".

Sarah Aaaronsohn and Avshalom Feinberg after his release from prison, Beersheba, January 1916.

Source: Institution Tamar Eshel

MATA HARI
Dutch Spy
(1876 – 1917)

Margaretha Geertruida Zelle was born in Leeuwarden, Holland on 7th August 1876. She was the eldest of four children and her parents ran a hat shop.

Until she was 13 when her Father went bankrupt, Margaretha enjoyed a life of luxury and went to expensive private schools.

Her Mother died in 1891 and her Father re-married, after which Margaretha went to live with her Godfather in Sneek.

When she was eighteen, Margaretha answered an advertisement placed in a Dutch newspaper by a man who lived in the Dutch East Indies and was looking for a wife. She married Rudolf MacLeod, a Dutch Colonial Army Captain of Scottish origin and moved to Malang on the east side of Java. They had two children – a boy and a girl but the marriage soon failed and Margaretha went to live with another officer, during which time she learnt Indonesian dancing and in 1897 chose the native name Mata Hari.

Mata ended up working as a dancer in Paris but by the time the war broke out, her career was virtually over. She was, however, very popular and had relationships with high-ranking military officers and politicians from many countries. As Holland remained neutral during WW1, Mata was able to travel freely.

She was suspected of being a spy for the Germans and arrested in 1916 and interrogated by the British but released without charge. In January 1917 she was again arrested – this time by the French - and this time was tried as a spy, found guilty and executed on 15th October 1917.

MISTINGUETT
French Entertainer
(1875 – 1956)

Born Jeanne Bourgeois at Enghien-les-Bains on 5th April 1875. Soon afterward the family moved to Soisy-sous-Montmorency where Jeanne grew up.

She studied dancing and singing and went to Paris to study the violin. During the journey, she met a man called Saint-Marcel who was in charge of the show at the Casino de Paris.

Finally settling on the stage name "Mistinguett" (which I am reliably informed involved a play on the English word Miss), Jeanne began working as a comedy singer at the Eldorado in Paris. In 1912, Jeanne worked with Maurice Chevalier at the Folies Bergère and they fell in love. Until 1914, Mistinguett also worked as an actress in silent films, soon becoming an international star and one of the highest paid female cabaret singers in the world.

During the First World War, Maurice Chevalier was wounded and taken prisoner by the Germans (again, I am reliably informed that when he was a PoW, Chevalier met the English actor Jack Warner – Dixon of Dock Green – who taught him English and learnt French). Mistinguett wanted to get Chevalier out of prison, so she volunteered to help the British Intelligence Service in Paris. Chevalier was freed in 1916 due to Mistinguett's relationship with King Alphonse XIII of Spain.

She died in Bougival, France at the age of 80 in 1956. The French author Jean Cocteau described her thus: "Her voice, slightly off-key, was that of the Parisian street hawkers."

JANET MORGAN

The
SECRETS
Of
RUE S₮ ROCH

Hope and Heroism Behind Enemy Lines
in the
First World War

LISE RISCHARD
Luxembourgish Spy
Died 1940

In her fantastic book "The Secrets of Rue St Roch. Intelligence Operations Behind Enemy Lines in the First World War", Janet Morgan tells the astonishing story of a very inspirational woman of World War One - Madame Lise Rischard.

Madame Rischard (née Meyer) was a housewife who lived in the city of Luxembourg, capital of the Grand Duchy of Luxembourg.

Many who live in the British Isles have scant knowledge of the large number of wars fought on the Continent of Europe. Following one such war (The Eighty Years War), Luxembourg became part of The Netherlands. In 1815 The Treaty of Paris declared Luxembourg an independent Grand Duchy

The Grand Duchy has borders with Germany, France and Belgium. From 1914 – 1918, Germany occupied the tiny country, which at that time had a population of 260,000.

Officially, Luxembourg was neutral during the 1914 – 1918 War and was ruled by Grand Duchess Marie-Adelaide. There was fierce fighting in that area in the Ardennes, Verdun and in the Vosges Mountains.

The City of Luxembourg is often referred to as the "Gibraltar of the North" due to the fact that the city was constructed on an outcrop of rock. Trains to France and Belgium from Germany run through Luxembourg, which meant the country played a pivotal role during the First World War.

Madame Rischard had one son – Marcel - from her first marriage to a Frenchman named Pelletier. Marcel was a keen sportsman and had been a member of the French Olympic Team at the Olympic Games held in Stockholm in 1912.

That was the first time that Luxembourg had entered a team for the modern Olympic games and the team consisted of just two athletes – Pelletier and a long jumper called Paul Fournelle. Marcel finished 17th in the shot put competition and 31st in the discus.

In the summer of 1916, Marcel was living in Paris. He sent a letter to his Mother asking her to visit him before he was sent to the Front.

Paris was not occupied by the Germans in the First World War and remained a free city for the duration of the War. However civilians even from neutral countries could not travel freely – travel from Luxembourg to France was via Switzerland (also neutral) and visas were required.

While she was in Paris to visit her son, Madame Rischard was approached by a British Intelligence Officer and recruited to help the Allied cause.

In her carefully researched book, Janet Morgan tells the astonishing story of what happened next, detailing the exploits of Madame Rischard during the First World War and how she and a small, dedicated band of people from Luxembourg risked their lives to help the Allied cause, undoubtedly making an extremely valuable contribution.

After the War, the incredible bravery and hard work of Madame Rischard and some of her fellow agents was recognised and they were awarded the Chevalier du Legion d'Honneur on the recommendation of Marshal Foch of the French Army. According to Morgan, they all also "received British decorations and French medals and in Madame Rischard's case, the French medal The Croix de Guerre with Palm" (p. 341).

"The Secrets of Rue St Roch. Intelligence Operations Behind Enemy Lines in the First World War" by Janet Morgan (London: Allen Lane, an imprint of Penguin Books, 2004).

MAY SINCLAIR
English Writer
(1863 – 1946)

Mary Amelia St Clair was born on 24th August 1863 in Rock Ferry on the Wirral Peninsular - the youngest of the six children and only daughter of wealthy Liverpool shipowner William Sinclair. May's father went bankrupt and died when May was in her teens. May and her family then moved to Ilford, near London. She attended Cheltenham Ladies College for a year before returning home to look after her brothers – four of whom died early deaths from heart defects.

In 1886, she published her first volume of poetry – "Nakiketas and Other Poems" - under the name Julian Sinclair but when she had to start earning a living from writing in order to support herself and her ailing mother, she adopted the penname for which she is best known - May Sinclair.

May was already a successful author well before the First World War period, having published numerous novels and collections of stories, as well as a highly respected biography of the Brontë Sisters called "The Three Brontës".

She was a keen supporter of the Suffragette movement and wrote pamphlets for the Woman Writers Suffrage League.

When World War One broke out, May joined Dr. Monro's Flying Ambulance and went to Belgium in September 1914. By then she was 52, which in those days, was 'old'.

Shortly afterwards, May returned to England suffering from shell shock and wrote about her experiences in *A Journal of Impressions in Belgium*, published in New York by Macmillan in 1915.

Three of May's nephews enlisted – two died and one spent much of the War as a prisoner of war and returned home ill with pneumonia. May nursed him back to health.

Sinclair was one of the early Modernists and, as well as her novels and literary critiques, also wrote non fiction on subjects varying from Imagism, Freudian psychology and German philosophical idealism.

In April 1918, May Sinclair was the first to use the term originally invented by psychologist William James "stream of consciousness" – or interior monologue – as a literary technique to describe Dorothy Richardson' s narration in the book "Pilgrimage" in a review that she was writing for "The Egoist" journal.

She was a prolific writer from the 1880s through until the late 1920s when she was diagnosed with Parkinson's disease and decided to give up writing. She retired to live in Buckinghamshire and died in Bierton on 14th November 1946.

PRINCESS PATRICIA OF CONNAUGHT
(1886 – 1974)

Did you know we had a Princess Patricia? Victoria Patricia Helena Elizabeth was one of Queen Victoria's granddaughters. She was born on 17th March 1886 in London.

Her Mother was Princess Louise Margaret of Prussia and her Father was Prince Arthur, Duke of Connaught and Strathearn, third son of Queen Victoria and Prince Albert of Saxe-Coburg and Gotha (no wonder the Royal Family changed their name during the First World War).

Princess Patricia was a bridesmaid at the wedding of the Duke and Duchess of York – the future King George V and Queen Mary.

Patricia travelled with her family to Canada in 1911 when her Father was appointed Governor General of Canada. Her portrait was on the One Dollar note of the Dominion of Canada issued in March 1917.

When the War broke out, Canada answered the call immediately. Montreal millionaire Andrew Hamilton Gault – who had served with the Royal Canadian Rifles in South Africa – decided to found a unit of elite troops who had already experienced action. He raised a regiment of light infantry and asked permission to use Princess Patricia's name. So Princess Patricia's Canadian Light Infantry came into being and the princess was their Colonel-in-Chief until her death.

She designed and embroidered a banner for the regiment to carry into battle She also designed the cap badge and collar badges for the regiment – depicting a single daisy, in honour of Hamilton Gault's wife Marguerite.

The Regiment attended and the band played at Princess Patricia's wedding in 1919 to commoner The Hon. Alexander Ramsay, after which she gave up her royal title and became Lady Patricia Ramsey.

The Princess Patricia's Light Infantry Regiment still exists in Canada today, with their HQ in Edmonton – www.ppcli.com

Photos
Previous Page: Official portrait of Princess Patricia
Next Page Top: Princess Patricia Presenting the Colours
Next Page Bottom: Unnamed members of PPCLI in England in 1914

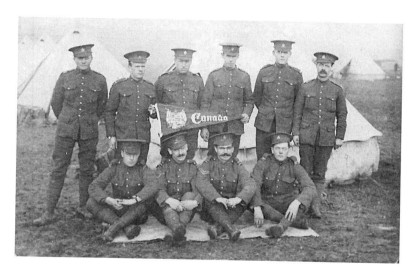

MOINA BELLE MICHAEL
American Professor & Humanitarian
(1869 – 1944)

Moina Belle Michael was born in Good Hope, Georgia on 15th August 1869. She trained as a teacher and taught at the University of Georgia but took leave of absence to travel and study in Europe.

She was teaching in Rome in Italy when war broke out and, while waiting for her passage home, she volunteered to help a Committee set up to help other American citizens stranded in Europe at that time. Moina managed to get a passage home on the *Carpathia* – the ship that had rescued survivors from the *Titanic*.

She then went to New York to undertake the training of YMCA workers who were to be sent overseas.

After the war, Moina returned to Georgia and among her pupils were disabled ex-servicemen newly returned from fighting in the First World War. First-hand experience of the aftermath of the Great War would have fuelled the idea of her poem:

Having read John McCrae's poem **'In Flanders Fields'**, Moina Michael made a personal pledge to 'keep the faith'.

She felt compelled to make a note of this pledge and hastily scribbled down a response entitled "We Shall Keep the Faith" on the back of a used envelope. From that day she vowed to wear a red poppy of Flanders Fields as a sign of remembrance.

The idea soon spread through Moina's meetings with fellow members of the YMCA Secretaries of the Allied Nations and in 1919 the fledgling Royal British Legion in the UK adopted the poppy as its emblem.

Moina Belle Michael died in Athens, Georgia on 10th May 1944 and, 4 years later, was commemorated on a postage stamp.

In 1969, the Georgia General Assembly designated the stretch of US Highway 78 between Athens and Monroe the "Moina Michael Highway" in her honour.

BEATRIX BRICE MILLER
English Writer & Red Cross VAD
(1877- 1959)

Beatrix was born in 1877 in Vilparaiso,Chile, of British parents – her Mother was Mary Brice Miller, nee Walker from Charlton, Kent. Beatrix was educated privately. When her Father died, the family returned to England and Beatrix lived in Goring-on-Thames and later Chelsea.

She served with the BEF, travelling to France in 1914 as a Red Cross VAD 'Lady Helper' (as opposed to a 'Trained Nurse'), following which she dedicated herself to ensuring the exploits of the brave 'Old Contemptibles' of the First Seven Divisions were not forgotten – that our debt to them be repaid and their memory honoured.

Beatrix wrote the poem "To the Vanguard" which was first published in The Times of 2nd November 1916 and which became among the best-remembered verses of the War. It also appeared in a small collection of Brice Miller's poems called "To The Vanguard And Other Songs To The Seven Divisions" which featured 8 poems and was dedicated "to the Fallen, the Disabled, the Prisoners and those still Fighting."

Beatrix and her Mother, Mary Louise Brice Miller were mentioned in Sir Douglas Haig's dispatch published in the London Gazette on 29th May 1917, among the names of the trained nurses and lady helpers to be honoured by the King in a special investiture in Hyde Park on 2nd June.

In December 1917, Beatrix organised a special pageant in the Royal Albert Hall to commemorate the battles of the original BEF and collaborated with General Sir William Pultenay in "The Immortal Salient" which was a record and guide to the Ypres Salient battlegrounds.

In 1922, Beatrix launched a campaign to raise awareness of the annual "Ypres Day" that she and fellow members of the "Ypres League" had started two years earlier - as she suggested in "The Times": "one day of the year we may unite in commemorating the Glory that is Ypres." She and fellow members of the "Ypres League" arranged to hold a ceremony on 30th October at the Cenotaph in Whitehall where people who had lost relatives or friends in the Salient could take part in a great floral tribute. The event was attended by Princess Beatrice, Queen Victoria's youngest daughter, who had herself lost a son in the Great War.

In 1937 Beatrix worked on a documentary for the BBC wireless about the fighting from Mons to Ypres from August to November 1914. According to The Times newspaper, this was broadcast in August 1939.

After her death in Chelsea, London, on 25th May 1959 at the age of 82, Beatrix left in her will a bequest to ensure the building of a memorial to the BEF, 1914.

An e-mail from David Reynolds, Beatrix Brice Miller's great nephew corrected my spelling of her name which he found through my weblog and continued:

"She wrote the poem that begins 'Oh little mighty force that stood for England…' in 1914 about the BEF. It became quite famous and was a favourite among the old soldiers of those regiments, nicknamed 'The Old Contemptibles". When she died, there was a memorial service at St. Martin in the Fields church. I was a child and don't remember much about it, except that the church was full of old soldiers in uniforms with medals."

TO THE VANGUARD

OH little mighty Force that stood for England !
That, with your bodies for a living shield,
Guarded her slow awaking, that defied
The sudden challenge of tremendous odds
And fought the rushing legions to a stand
Then stark in grim endurance held the line.
O little Force that in your agony
Stood fast while England girt her armour on,
Held high our honour in your wounded hands,
Carried our honour safe with bleeding feet
We have no glory great enough for you,
The very soul of Britain keeps your day !
Procession ? Marches forth a Race in Arms ;
And, for the thunder of the crowd's applause,
Crash upon crash the voice of monstrous guns,
Fed by the sweat, served by the life of England,
Shouting your battle cry across the world.

Oh, little mighty Force, your way is ours,
This land inviolate your monument.

Poem previously published in "To The Vanguard And Other Songs To The Seven Divisions" by Beatrix Brice Miller (London: Bickers & Sons, 1917)

Internet Research Sources: "The Times" Archive 1959-06-24 and "British Journal of Nursing", 2nd July 1917.

KATHLEEN SCOTT
English Sculptor
(1878 – 1947)

Kathleen Scott, nee Bruce, was born on 27th March 1878 at Carlton-in-Lindrick, near Worksop. On her Mother Janie's side, Kathleen's grandparents were James Skene the watercolour painter and Rhalou Rizo-Rangabe who was Greek. Kathleen's father was the Reverend Lloyd Bruce, a descendant of Robert the Bruce of Scotland.

In 1901 Kathleen went to Paris, where she studied with Rodin the sculptor and met Gertrude Stein the American poet, Isadora Duncan the dancer, whose daughter Kathleen helped to deliver, and other celebrities of the time such as George Bernard Shaw, who she later sculpted, and Edward Steichen (the photographer, painter and art gallery curator).

In December 1903 Kathleen went to Salonika with the Macedonia Relief Fund to help out. She contracted Typhoid Fever while there. In 1906 - 1907 Kathleen travelled to Greece to find her roots. She met Captain Scott in the Autumn of 1907 in London and they were married on 2nd September 1908.

Kathleen travelled to New Zealand to see her husband off on his ill-fated expedition to the South Pole. In January 1913, she was on her way to meet him when Scott died but the news did not reach her until 19th February because wireless was still not widely used in ships at that time. Kathleen, left to bring up their son alone, shouldered the task with impressive stoicism – she had many friends who were very supportive.

During the First World War, Kathleen 'involved herself in war work. She drove cars and ambulances to France, helped at a hospital, organised volunteers among her friends and raised money. She was close friends with Violet Asquith, daughter of the British Prime Minister, who went with her to France.

Back in London, Kathleen worked at the Vickers factory in Erith making electrical coils. She was popular with her fellow workers and took 40 of them in an outing to see "Peter Pan". She was the confidante of Herbert Asquith and close friends with J.M. Barrie, George Bernard Shaw, Geoffrey Dearmer and T.E. Lawrence, who she also sculpted.

Towards the end of 1917, Kathleen travelled to Paris where she experienced daily bombardments from the huge German gun known as 'Big Bertha'. Back in London in October 1918, Kathleen had an interview at Ellerman's Hospital to see about helping the surgeons repair the facial wounds of servicemen.

She made models of the men's faces, recreated the missing parts so the surgeons could work without having to experiment on the men. Kathleen's former professor at the Slade – Henry Tonks – led the way with this pioneering work, which Kathleen felt was the most important she had done to date.

In November 1919 Kathleen met Edward Hilton Young, who was a barrister who had joined the Navy during WW1, commanded an armoured train in Russia and lost an arm during the Zebrugge raid. They fell in love, married, had a son of their own - Wayland - and lived happily until Kathleen's death on 24th July 1947.

Source: YOUNG, Louisa "A Great Task of Happiness - The life of Kathleen Scott" (Macmillan, London, 1995).

Louisa Young is Weyland Young's daughter – Kathleen's Granddaughter. Her book is wonderful – do read it.

Kathleen with Robert Falcon Scott

Kathleen Scott's statue of Captain Scott in New Zealand

BETTY STEVENSON
English YMCA Worker
(1896 – 1917)

Betty was born Bertha Grace Stevenson in York on 3rd September
1896.   Her father was Arthur G. Stevenson and her mother
Catherine Grace Stvenson. The family later moved to Harrogate to a
house called "Grey Gables".   She went to boarding school in 1910
and to Brussels to study music in 1913. When war broke out, Betty
and her family helped out with Belgian Refugee families, some of
whom her family took in.   During that time, she learnt to drive.

In January 1916, one of Betty's aunts went to manage a YMCA Canteen at St. Denis in France. Although she was considered too young at nineteen, Betty persevered and eventually got permission to go. As she had always written letters and kept diaries, Betty continued to do so while in France. She described the rough crossing of the Channel and having to wear a life jacket.

Betty and her aunt lived in the Hotel Magenta in the Boulevard Magenta in Paris, which was about two kilometres from the Gare du Nord and the Gare de l'Est. The hotel only provided breakfast - hot chocolate, bread, apricot jam and brioche - and Betty had to find her own evening meal.

Betty's Aunt had to go back to England so it was decided that Betty's Mother, Grace, should replace her and on 30th March 1916, Betty's Mother joined her in Paris. She had been going to travel on the SS Sussex but her plans were changed which was fortuitous as the Sussex was torpedoed.

The YMCA Hut the pair worked in was at Saint-Denis, due north of Paris, and they travelled to work by tram. The Hut was in the middle of a cinder road in a compound with Motor Transport workshops where vehicles from the front were repaired. YMCA volunteers worked either from 9am till 3pm or from 5pm until 10pm. In Betty's Mother's words the YMCA Huts were "little lifeboats on a sea of warfare" providing refreshments etc for the soldiers. (p. 70)

When Betty and her Aunt first went out the hut was very ill equipped. The only stove was at the opposite end to the counter, the water seldom boiled and every drop of it had to be carried from one end of the hut to the other. After a few weeks, Betty and her Aunt procured a better stove and a quantity of pipes and the men who worked in the Motor Transport workshops installed it all. A Frenchwoman whose husband had been killed in 1915 helped the Englishwomen.

Initially, YMCA volunteers did not wear a uniform, which apparently went down well with the men who were sick and tired of uniforms. Instead, they wore a special YMCA sash which ensured them safe passage wherever they went. Later on in the war, they work khaki serge skirts and jackets with khaki blouses.

Travel to and from the Hut in Saint-Denis was "a nightmare. Sometimes we waited from half an hour to an hour and a half in all weathers at a corner close to our hotel for the tram which was always crowded. After the night shift the trams had stopped running and we had to walk to the nearest station and get a train to the Gare du Nord, which took ages. Walking through the station, we had to be careful not to step on sleeping *Poilus* (as the French soldiers were called in WW1) on leave, lying dead asleep, coated with mud and laden with kit, straight from the trenches."

Although the windows of their room looked onto to a noisy Boulevard, "there was a chestnut tree just outside, in whose branches a pair of pigeons built a nest on a level with our window". On Sundays there were "lots of our own men walking about and making the most of Paris leave." (pp. 71 - 73).

Kind friends raised £100 and the YMCA put up £50 so Betty and her Mother were able to purchase a small Ford car which meant they no longer had to rely on public transport. The vehicle they chose was "light on tyres and petrol". They were thus able to approach their work with greater energy as they were not tired out from the journey to work and back. Betty's younger brother, Arthur, joined them to help out during the Easter school holidays.

Measles broke out in the camp and Betty and Arthur both came down with it. The Hut was closed and out of bounds for a fortnight while Mrs Stevenson looked after her children with the help of an Army Medical Officer and the loan of an ambulance from a Captain Rankin from time to time, so they could go out without risking infecting anyone else.

By 15th May, the hut was re-opened and Betty and her mother went back to work - much to the relief of all who used it as the facilities had been sorely missed. All was not work, however. One evening they went to the Alhambra theatre to see a show featuring "ventriloquists, singers, dancers, trick cyclists, impersonators and a man with a performing alligator" (p. 77).

On 16th June, Betty and her Mother received a letter from Lady Bessborough with a special message from Princess Helena Victoria, thanking them for their invaluable work at St. Denis.

Betty's Mother went to see the Scottish Women's Hospital at Royaumont, which was run by Dr. Frances Ivens. Grace was so impressed by what she saw that she and Betty endowed a bed at the hospital. Dr. Ivens sent some of her staff to Paris to visit Betty on 22nd June.

Afterwards, Betty drove her guests back to the hospital and described the drive back to Paris "along the edge of the great forest with gypsies encamped there.

The guns were making a great noise" and Betty said she would never forget that drive. "This was the preparation for the Battle of the Somme which began eight days later. " (p. 83).

In July 1916, Betty and her Mother were sent off on leave. They went to Finistere in Brittany, where Betty's Father and brother joined them. While there, they were offered a more exciting job but Betty voted to stay with the people who knew them so well at Saint-Denis. That winter was hard "The cold in October and November was the worst I had ever known. We had, for a long time, no coal or wood in the hotel and fires were out of the question until we managed to get hold of some logs. We wrapped coats around our feet and legs and occasionally we would go out and take a ride on a tram or in the Metro, where there was always 'a good dug on'. The nights were were frightfully cold and everything in the room froze."

Their time was up at the end of November 1916 and they returned home across the Channel, the journey taking 32 hours from Le Havre to Southampton in a 'violent storm'. (pp. 89 - 90).

Betty remained in England from November 1916 until April 1917 when she decided to 'go back to her beloved Tommies, this time as a motor driver." (p. 91). She travelled to Boulogne and was billeted in a town about nineteen miles away in a large house next to a cinema with other YMCA volunteers and an Army Officer. There was a YMCA hostel where they could have baths at the other end of the town. Unable to comment further due to censorship, Betty's letter to her Mother says that everything is "simply teeming with interest".

Anzac Day 1917 (25th April) was celebrated with "great doings all the day and sports and football matches galore" and "thousands of Australians just marched past". Betty also mentioned the cemetery with it's average of 40 burials per day.

On 12th May 1917, Betty described seeing "...an air fight and a Taube was brought down. A piece of our own Archie shell fell just outside the YMCA Hut, an enormous piece". She also described going to other camps where she could hear the guns and see the flashes (pp. 108 - 111).

Betty's duties as a driver varied from driving relatives to visit the wounded in hospitals or to attend funerals, delivering entertainers to Huts, driving people to the port to catch ferries and, of course, servicing her car.

"If there don't happen to be any relatives to ferry, I report to Stores" driving rations to various Huts in camps within a ten or twelve mile radius of her base - "in fact, driving anything and everything all day and half the night".

"When I say 'hospital', I expect you imagine a big building but they are only tents, sometimes a wooden hut, planted along the side of the road with the railway and ambulance sidings at the back" (p.127).

There were no women workers in the YMCA Huts nearer to the front line - sometimes because of a lack of suitable living accommodation, sometimes because 'women were not allowed there'. Occasionally, Betty had to drive a lecturer with his assistants and projector to some far flung YMCA Huts.

When it rained, the area was turned into mud and the girls wore "gum boots" (Wellington boots). Betty asked her Mother to get her a mac that didn't let the rain in - something called a "Quorn". She described the rain as "extraordinary - in an hour the roads are nearly a foot deep in water and mud." (pp 152 - 153).

"I have been getting up at 5 am and going to the sidings to sell things to the men going up the line". This work understandably upset Betty but she forced herself to be cheerful and make jokes for the sake of the Tommies. There was a "little shanty at the sidings which is open till 9 am" - drinks, magazines and newspapers were free.

One of Betty's fellow drivers was a man who was a Commissioned Officer who had been badly wounded and had shell shock which left him with a very bad stammer - sometimes he had to write down what he wanted to say.

Unable to get home as planned for her 21st birthday, Betty celebrated with friends on 3rd September 1917, arriving in London on 4th September in the middle of an air raid.

Her birthday celebrations in Harrogate lasted three days. Then she had some leave and time to rest, returning to France on Saturday, 6th October 1917.

Betty described the coats she wore for coping with the cold "Leather Coat, British Warm, Mackintosh, 2 scarves" (p. 166 - 167). On 11th November 1917, Betty wrote to tell her Mother that they were to have one fixed half-day off each week.

By 17th December, after another bout of 'flu, Betty was transferred from driving back to canteen work. Her superiors had wanted to send her home for a good long rest but she didn't want to go. She described the Hut - for the Canadian troops - at Christmas "decorated with holly, mistletoe and evergreens and big red tissue paper bows and red berries. For the evening we had a Christmas tree and Father Christmas. Every man got a present from the tree, a bag of sweets and tobacco and a Christmas card. All the food and drinks were free. Then we had a band and a concert and dance. Our Hut is only one of about thirty and they all had similar entertainment." (p. 195).

When her car was off the road, Betty drove a horse and cart to deliver supplies to Huts - the horse, an old Artillery horse, was called Flying Fox and together they had lots of adventures, much to the amusement of those who knew Betty driving her Ford motorcar.

Betty's last leave home began on 21st February 1918 and she reached home in Harrogate on 22nd February. On 15th March Betty and her Mother went to spend some fun time in London. "Betty was eighteen when the war began" explained her Mother "just the age when most girls look forward to, and get, all sorts of fun and 'good times' and Betty loved these things." (p. 224).

No YMCA female workers were allowed to return to their work in France during the German push which began on 21st March 1918, however by 7th May, Betty was off again to join her fellow YMCA volunteers working in a YMCA Hut in Etaples, France.

Thousands of refugees flooded through Etaples and after her work in the canteen, night after night Betty and her fellow volunteers went to help, distributing food and drink to the refugees at the station. On the way back to their quarters on the night of 30th May, the party were caught in an air raid and took shelter behind a hedge. In spite of wearing a tin hat, when an enemy plane jettisoned his bombs in open countryside, Betty was hit and fatally wounded, dying instantly.

She was buried with full military honours in the British military cemetery at Etaples and was awarded the French Croix de Guerre avec Palme.

After the war Betty's Mother and Aunt put together a book using Betty's diaries and letters home. At the end of the book are letters from people who knew and loved Betty. There can be no better memorial to her than this one from one of the lecturers she drove, referred to as 'Mr M':

Mr M said that during the course of his lecture there was a very bad raid and he assumed that he would have to stay the night. However, when he suggested this, he was told "Miss Stevenson will be here in twenty minutes" and sure enough she was soon "threading her way through the shell-holes and broken ground". She drove Mr M back to his billet and he asked Betty "Are you bound to come out when it's like this"? Betty said she did not know what Mr M meant, so he tried again "Do men order you to come out when there is a raid on? "No", she said, "they don't order us but of course we come." (pp. 294 - 195).

Source: "Betty Stevenson, YMCA Croix de Guerre avec Palme Sept. 3rd 1896 - May 30th 1918"
Edited by G.G.R.S. and A.G.S. published by Longmans Green and Company, New York, 1920

MUNITIONS WORKERS

A shortage of artillery shells had been a serious problem to the British Army since the Autumn of 1914. In May 1915, the Times newspaper war correspondent Colonel Charles à Court Repington sent a telegram to his newspaper in which he complained about the lack of shells.

After the first Zeppelin raids on the British mainland and with a German submarine blockade of the British Isles, and having suffered three times as many casualties as the Germans at the Second Battle of Ypres, it became clear that the British needed a great many more shells if the Allies were to continue to fight the war.

In order to remedy the lack of ammunition, the British Government passed The Munitions of Work Act in 1915, which brought all munitions factories in Britain under the control of the Government. A Ministry of Munitions was set up under the leadership of Lloyd George and they began to build munitions factories.

Due to the great number of men who had enlisted in the armed forces, there was a need for women to volunteer to work in Munitions

Factories. In total, 947,000 women were employed in munitions work to manufacture bullets, shells and other military equipment. 300 of them died because of TNT poisoning or explosions during that time.

In 1917, The 'London Gazette' conducted a survey of 444,000 women - 68% had changed jobs since the beginning of the War - 16% moved from domestic service, 22% had been unemployed in early 1914 and now had jobs and 23% had moved from one factory to another. The survey explained that such a movement of women workers had not been seen prior to WW1.

Sir Arthur Conan Doyle paid a secret visit to the Gretna Factory in 1918 and it was he who coined the term "Devil's Porridge" when he saw the mixture of nitro-glycerine and gun-cotton that turned into a sort of paste.

EUPHEMIA CUNNINGHAM
English Munitions Worker
(1892 – 1989)

There were thousands of women who worked in Munitions Factories during the First World War. The work was difficult and dangerous. The girls risked their lives, breathing in toxic fumes that turned their skin yellow, giving rise to the popular nickname 'canary girls'. Unlike now, there was little protective clothing and we did not know then such chemicals could have a lasting, detrimental effect on the health of those who worked with them.

There were many well-documented accidents involving high explosives which claimed the lives of workers The most famous of which were the Silvertown explosion in London in 1917 where 73 were killed and more than 400 injured and the National Shell Filling Factory, Chilwell in which more than 130 workers died.

Among the many women who volunteered to work in munitions factories, here is just one story.

Euphemia was born in Edinburgh in 1892, the second daughter of Mr and Mrs William Cunningham. She was employed at the Gretna Factory from 15th August 1916 until 29th August 1919. She worked as a Forewoman at Hill 2, Nitro Glycerine Section, Broomhills Dornock.

In 1918, Euphemia was awarded the OBE 'for courage and high example in continuing her duties immediately after a severe explosion' at the factory. The ceremony was reported in the Scotsman newspaper and in The Times.

Euphemia married on 30th December 1921 in St. Giles Church, Edinburgh and we understand she later went to live in Australia.

Information supplied by The Devil's Porridge which is a museum dedicated to the story of HM Factory Gretna situated at Daleside, Butterdales, Eastriggs DG12 6TQ between Gretna and Annan, Solway in Scotland.

See their website at www.devilsporridge.co.uk

THE DICK, KERR'S LADIES FOOTBALL TEAM

Producing WW1 armaments at the Dick, Kerrs Factory in Preston

Many people these days think of ladies football as having started in the UK during the1970s but that is far from the truth. Allow me to introduce you to The Dick, Kerr's Ladies Football Team whose prowess at football raised huge sums of money for the war effort and surely earns them a place under the banner of Inspirational Women of WW1.

In the north of England, where the factories and mills of the Industrial Revolution undoubtedly contributed to putting the Great into Britain, girls played football like their brothers. So it is not surprising that the first women's football team began in Preston, Lancashire at the Dick, Kerr's Factory.

W.B. Dick and Co. had built trams and in 1883 got together with John Kerr and acquired premises in Preston in 1893 – they made the famous open-topped trams, which are now collectors' items. During the First World War the factory added munitions to their already considerable list of locomotives, cable drums, pontoon bridges, wagons, cartridge boxes, horseshoes, pontoon boats and seaplanes.

Due to the large numbers of men required to fight during the First World War – conscription first for unmarried men aged between the ages of 18 and 41 then for married men as well was brought in during 1916 – women had to go to work in order to keep the home fires burning. By 1917, the factory was turning out 3,000 shells a week.

The female workers joined the male apprentices during their lunch breaks for informal football games. After winning a match played against the men of the factory, the girls formed a women's football team. Their manager was a man called Alfred Frankland, from Fulwood in Preston, a former manager of a tailor's who volunteered for Army duty at the beginning of the War.

Frankland was in his thirties, married with a young son. He was also a born organiser and a natty dresser – always wearing a bowler hat, alpaca overcoat and a suit with waistcoat, complete with fob watch. A keen amateur sportsman, Frankland had noticed the games of football from his office window and offered to help.

On Christmas Day 1917, Dick, Kerr's Ladies played a charity match at Deepdale (home of Preston North End FC) in Preston in aid of the hospital for wounded soldiers at Moor Park, Preston. They played against Arundel Coulthard Factory and won 4 : 0. Ten thousand people watched that match and £488 7s was raised - but don't' forget there was no television in those days!

The scorers were Whittle, Birkins, Rance (2)

Dick, Kerr (b/w stripes): E. Clayton, B. Traynor, E. Nixon, E. Birkins, A. Kells, M. Kay, A. Standing, G. Whittle, F. Rance, F. Redford, L. Jones

Coulthards (r/w stripes): A. Sumner, May Coates, N. Charnley, J. Rangeley, L. Forshaw, F. Proudfoot, G. Fitzgerald, L. Atkinson, L. Rayton, L. Billington

*Dick, Kerrs' Ladies Team before their first ever match
on 25th December 1917 at Deepdale*

The girls went on to play similar games around the country, raising large sums of money for injured servicemen both during and after WW1. They received ten shillings towards their costs for each game played. In those days ten shillings was half of £1 (there were twenty shillings in a pound), which was the average wage for a worker.

The team colours were black and white striped jerseys with a small Union Jack. Later, the team's star players were Lily Parr and Alice Woods, both from St. Helens, who were stars in their day as the matches were featured regularly in Pathe news films.

In 1920, Dick, Kerr's Ladies Football Team played the first women's international football match against France, who fielded a team from Paris headed by Alice Milliat the French athlete. For International games the girls wore white jerseys and blue shorts with striped hats to cover their hair.

The girls went on to tour France and on Boxing Day 1920 they played in front of a crowd of 53,000 at Goodison Park against a team from St. Helens. In 1922, they toured Canada and the United States to great acclaim – travelling by boat from Liverpool. In those pre-Jumbo Jet days, ships left England every day bound for New York, Quebec and Montreal.

Although the team continued to play in one form or another until 1965, the Football Association became concerned about the popularity of the women's games and banned them from playing on F.A. grounds. Fortunately the girls were still able to play on grounds not controlled by the FA.

In 1926, following an argument with Alfred Frankland, the team's name was changed to Preston Ladies FC and the girls continued to play to crowds averaging 5,000 people.

The FA finally recognised women's football in 1971 and many teams now have successful women's teams so let's hear it for the girls who play football.

Source:
"The Dick, Kerr's Ladies The Factory Girls who took on the World" by Barbara Jacobs, published by Constable & Robinson Ltd. London, 2004.

COMPANION BOOK ALSO AVAILABLE!

"I like the way you include photos of the poets - this seems somehow to bring the book together and give one a real feel for what the times and the lives of the poets must have been like during WW1.

Elliott, Merseyside.

**Female Poets Of The First World War
Volume 1**
Compiled by Lucy London

Features short biographies, photos and examples of poetry from: Stella Benson (GB), Winifred Holtby (GB), Ella Wheeler Wilcox (USA), Jean Blewett (Canada), Akiko Yosano (Japan), Amalia Guglielminetti (Italy), Florbela Espanca (Portugal)

And many more besides...

Available now! Price £5.00 + p&p
Mail order from www.poshupnorth.com
ISBN: 978-1-909643-02-4

If you have enjoyed this book, why not have a look at our wider selection of publications embracing poetry, sports and other fascinating subjects. There are new additions to the range being added all the time, so do keep an eye on the website!

SELECTED POEMS 2012
Over 50 Of The Best Entries
From The 2012 Pendle War
Poetry Competition
Edited by Paul Breeze
ISBN 978-0-9539782-7-4
74 pages paperback
Selling Price: £5.00

Purple Patches
A collection of poems,
songs and short stories
from the fountain pen of
Lucy London
ISBN: 978-1-909643-00-0
42 pages paperback
Selling Price £4.00

Guns & Pencils
An Anthology Of War
Poetry
By Lucy London
ISBN: 978-0-9539782-2-9
26 pages paperback
Selling Price: £4.00

**Blackpool To Bond
Street!**
The fascinating story of
Amy Blackburn – pioneer
of the makeover
By Joan Shaw
ISBN: 978-0-9539782-5-0
60 pages paperback
Selling Price: £6.00

Full details can be found at www.poshupnorth.com

ISAAC ROSENBERG (1890-1918)
£92.000 Appeal To Finance A Commemorative Statue

Isaac Rosenberg, one of the greatest of the First World War poets and a talented artist, has not received the widespread recognition he deserves.

The son of Jewish Lithuanian immigrants, he grew up in deprived circumstances in London's East End and was obliged to leave school at 14 to work. Thanks to Birkbeck College, however, where the fees were modest and the standards high, he was able to continue his studies at night. During his years at Birkbeck's art department (1907-1911), he received a sound training, won several prizes and produced his earliest-known self-portrait, now at Tate Britain. This same rigorous training enabled him to win a place at the Slade School of Fine Art, University College, London, which he attended from 1911 to 1914. He was staying with his sister, Minnie, in Cape Town when war broke out

That put an end to Rosenberg's hopes of earning a living through painting or writing. In 1915 he enlisted in the British army. He was killed near Arras on April 1, 1918, in the great German offensive. His remains are unidentified to this day and his only real memorial is a gravestone in France recording his name and his profession, 'Artist and Poet'.

It is proposed that the statue will be in Torrington Square on the Birkbeck College campus. The proximity to the two great learning centres in Rosenberg's life, Birkbeck and the Slade, make this an even more fitting memorial to his genius.The statue will be only the fifth statue of a poet in London and only the second in Britain of a Jewish literary figure (the other being Benjamin Disraeli).

Payments to: Jeecs-Rosenberg Statue appeal, c/o Clive Bettington, P.O. Box 57317, London E1 3WG www.jeecs.org.uk/rosenberg

THE DEVIL'S PORRIDGE

Daleside, Butterdales Road, Eastriggs, Annan,
Dumfries and Galloway, DG12 6TU

Eastriggs and Gretna Heritage have launched a fundraising campaign to raise £50,000 for a statue and memorial to commemorate the contribution made by women in two world wars.

The statue of a munitions girl will be erected at the new Devil's Porridge Museum which is set to open in 2014, in time to commemorate the centenary of World War One.

The Devil's Porridge tells the amazing story of "the greatest factory on earth" where 30,000 women and men came from all over to produce cordite. 12,000 female workers mixed the volatile explosive by hand and did their bit to win the war and gain votes for women.

We are seeking small and large donations to be gift-aided to our cause. We are also seeking charitable trust support to make our project possible.

Please send donations made payable to Eastriggs and Gretna Heritage, (Scottish Charity No. SC031616.), c/o 2 Blake Terrace, Dornock Annan Dumfriesshire DG12 6SR

We welcome questions by e-mail to our Chairman Richard Brodie to: richardrbrod@aol.com

For more information about the Devil's Porridge museum, visit the website at
www.devilsporridge.co.uk

BIBLIOGRAPHY

BOOKS

ADIE, Kate.- "Fighting on the Home Front The Legacy of Women in World War One". (Hodder & Stoughton, London, 2013)

ADDINGTON, Scott. "Heroes of the Line" (Scott Addington, 2013)

ALAN, A.J.- "Second Book". (Hutchinson & Co. Ltd., London, 1932)

ANDERSON, Ross. - "The Forgotten Front The East African Campaign". (Tempus Publishing Ltd., Stroud, Gloucestershire, 2004)

ATKINSON, Diane..- "Elsie and Mairi go to War Two Extraordinary Women on the Western Front". (Preface Publishing, London, 2009)

BAMFORD, Joe. - "Surviving the Skies A Night Bomber Pilot in the Great War". (Spelmount, an imprint of The History Press, Stroud, Gloucestershire, 2012)

BARKER, Pat.- "The Regeneration Trilogy – Regeneration, The Eye in the Door and The Ghost Road". (Viking, London, 1995)

BATTISCOMBE, Georgina. "Queen Alexandra". (Sphere Books, Falmouth, 1972)

BELBEN, Rosalind.- "Our Horses in Egypt" (Vintage, London, 2008)

BENTLEY, James. Ed.- "Some Corner of a Foreign Field Poetry of the Great War". (Little, Brown & Co., London, 1992)

BILTON, David .- "Images of War The Germans in Flanders 1914". (Pen & Sword, Barnsley, 2012)

BIRN, Antony and BIRN, Nicholas. Eds.- "Voices from the Front Line'. (Summersdale Publishers Ltd., Chichester, Sussex, 2008)

BOORMAN, Derek.- "A Century of Remembrance. 100 Outstanding British War Memorials". (Pen & Sword Books, Barnsley, Yorkshire, 2005)

CARDINAL, Agnes, GOLDMAN, Dorothy, HATTAWAY, Judith. Eds..- "Women's Writing on the First World War". (Oxford University Press, Oxford, 1999)

CLARKE, G.H. Ed.- "A Treasury of War Poetry British and American Poems 1914 – 1919". (Hodder & Stoughton, London, 1917)

COWEN, Ruth, Ed.- "A Nurse at the Front The Great War Diaries of Sister Edith Appleton". (Simon & Schuster, London, 2012)

CROSS, George Herbert. "Suffolk Punch - A Businessman's Autobiography". (Faber and Faber, London, 1936)

CHURCHILL, Winston.- "The Second World War Book I The Gathering Storm from War to War 1919 – 1939" (Cassell & Co. Ltd., London, 1967)

DEARBORN, Mary V.- "Queen of Bohemia The Life of Louise Bryant". (Houghton Mifflin Company, Boston, 1996)

DEPP, Wolfgang G., MIDDLETON, Christopher, SCHONHERR, Herbert. Eds. - "Ohne Hass und Fahne No Hatred and no Flag Sans haine et sans drapeau". (Rowohlt, Hamburg, 1959)

DOWSON, Jane, Ed. -"Women's Poetry of the 1930s A Critical Anthology". (Routledge, London, 1996)

FAULKS, Sebastian.- "Birdsong". (Vintage, London, 1994)

FOWLER WRIGHT. S.- Ed. - "Poets of Merseyside An Anthology of Present Day Poetry". (Merton Press Ltd., London, 1923)

GOLDSTEIN, Joshua S.- "War and Gender: How Gender shapes the War System and Vice Versa". (Cambridge University Press, Cambridge, 2001)

GOODWIN, Daisy, Ed.- "The Nation's Favourite Love Poems". (BBC Books, London, 1998)

GOSSE, Philip. - "A Naturalist goes to War being the Memoirs of a Camp-follower". (Penguin Books, London, 1944)

GRAVES, Diane. "A Crown of Life The World of John McCrae" (Spellmount Ltd., Staplehurst, Kent, 1997)

GRAVES, Robert.- "Goodbye to all that". (First published 1929)

HARRIS, Clive and WHIPPY, Julian. - "The Greater Game Sporting Icons who fell in the Great War".- (Pen and Sword Military, Barnsley, South Yorkshire, 2008)

HIBBERD, Dominic and ONIONS, John. Eds..- "The Winter of the World Poems of the First World War", (Constable and Robinson Ltd., London, 2007)

HIGGONET, Margaret, Ed. "Lines of Fire Women Writers of World War I". (Penguin Books, London, 1999)

HOLLIS, Matthew and KEEGAN, Paul, Eds.- "101 Poems against War". (Faber and Faber, London, 2003)

HOLT, Tonie and Valmai and ZEEPVAT, Charlotte, Eds. – "Poets of the Great War". (Pen & Sword Books Ltd., Barnsley, Yorkshire, 1999)

HOLTBY, Winifred. – "The Frozen Earth and other poems". (Collins, London, 1935)

JAMES, Lawrence.- "The Life and Legend of Lawrence of Arabia The Golden Warrior". (Weidenfield and Nicolson, London, 1990)

KHAN, Nosheen, Ed.. "Women's Poetry of the First World War". (Lexington, University Press of Kentucky, 1988)

LARKIN, Philip..- "The Oxford Book of Twentieth Century Verse Chosen by Philip Larkin". (Oxford University Press, Oxford, 1973)

LEWIS, Cecil.- "Sagittarius Rising". (Originally published by Peter Lewis, London, 1936. Pen and Sword, Barnsley, 2009)

LINTIER, Paul.- "My Seventy-Five The Journal of a French Gunner August – September 1914".

LLWYD, Alan, Ed. - "Out of the Fire of Hell. Welsh Experiences of the Great War 1914 – 1918 in prose and verse". (Gomer Press, Llandysal, Ceredigion SA4 4JL, 2008)

MACDONALD, John with ZELIKO, Cimpric. - "Caporetto and the Isonzo Campaign The Italian Front 1915 – 1918". (Pen & Sword Military, Barnsley, Yorkshire, 2011)

NOAKES, Vivien, Ed. - "Voices of Silence The Alternative Book of First World War Poetry". (Sutton Publishing Ltd., Stroud, Gloucestershire, 2006)

ODHAMS PRESS LTD. -"Fifty Amazing Stories of the Great War". (Odhams Press Ltd., London, 1936)

ODHAMS PRESS LTD. - "Fifty True Stories Stranger than Fiction". (Odhams Press Ltd., London, 1936)

POLE, Stephen and WHEAL, Elizabeth-Anne Eds. - "Dictionary of the First World War". (Pen & Sword Military Classics, Barnsley, Yorkshire, 2003)

POWELL, Anne, Ed. - "A Deep Cry". (Palladour Books, Aberporth, Wales, 1993)

POWELL, Anne.- "Women in the War Zone Hospital service in the First World War". (The History Press, Stroud, Gloucs., 2009)

REILLY, Catherine. Ed. - "Scars upon my Heart". (Virago Press, London, 1981)

REILLY, Catherine W. Ed. - "English Poetry of the First World War A Bibliography". (St. Martin's Press, Inc., New York, 1978)

ROBERTS, David, Ed.- "Minds at War Poetry and Experience of the First World War" (Saxon Books, Burgess Hill, 2010)

ROBERTS, David, Ed.- "Out in the Dark Poetry of the First World War" (Saxon Books, Burgess Hill, 1998)

SMITH, William James, Ed. – "Granger's Index to Poetry". (Columbia University Press, London, 1973).

SPRIET, Chris, Ed. -"We werden honderd jaar ouder (We aged a hundred years)". (Davidsfonds Uitgeverij, Leuven, 2013)

STALWORTHY, Jon. Ed.- "The Poems of Wilfred Owen". (Chatto & Windus, London, 1990)

YOUNG, Louisa.- "A Great Task of Happiness The Life of Kathleen Scott". (Macmillan, London, 1995)

WHITEHOUSE, Arch.- "The Zeppelin Fighters". (New English Library, London, 1972)

ZUBER, Terence.- "The Battle of the Frontiers Ardennes 1914". (Tempus Publishing Ltd., Stroud, Gloucestershire, 2007)

INTERNET SITES

http://oldpoetry.com/Madeline_Ida__Bedford__poems
http://www.firstworldwar.com/poetsandprose/sinclair.htm
http://www.greatwardifferent.com/Great_War/Nurses_6/Sinclair_01.htm
http://english.siu.edu/Resources/World%20War%20I%20Women%20Poets.pdf
http://members.home.nl/ja.goris/poetrywwl.htm
http://sophie.byu.edu/?q=node/3326
http://www.scuttlebuttsmallchow.com
http://www.firstworldwar.com/features/womenww1
http://www.spartacus.schoolnet.co.uk/Wbagnold.htm
http://www.amisldm.org/bibliographie/26-11-08-p-izquierdo/
http://fr.wikipedia.org/wiki/Marguerite_Durand_(féministe)
http://fr.wikipedia.org/wiki/Marguerite_Audoux
http://fr.wikipedia.org/wiki/Colette_Yver

http://fr.wikipedia.org/wiki/Lucie_Delarue-Mardrus
http://allpoetry.com/poem/8610927-_A_Fight_to_a_Finish_-by-S_Gertrude_Ford
http://www.whscms.org.uk/index.php?category_id=1994
The First World War Poetry Digital Archive, University of Oxford
www.oucs.ox.ac.uk/www1lit
www.poets.org

ACKNOWLEDGEMENTS

Dean Johnson of the Wilfred Owen Story museum and Janet Holmes of Rathbone Studio, Argyle Street, Birkenhead – for asking me to research female poets of the First World War for an exhibition and for their continued support

Paul who edits the exhibition panels and books – for his endless patience, perseverance, encouragement and wise advice – without him none of this would be possible

Dr. Margaret Stetz, Mae and Robert Carter Professor of Women's Studies and Professor of Humanities, University of Delaware, Newark, USA

Jenny Bartlett, Librarian, North London Collegiate School www.nlcs.org.uk

Elaine Edwards, Senior Curator, National Museums Scotland

Amy Goodwin, Salford Museum and Art Gallery

Mark Booth of Printwise, Poulton-le-Fylde for his patience and wonderful work

The Daily Mail
Bel Mooney
Kate Adie
Jeremy Paxman
Sir Hew Strachan
Professor Pierre Virey, France
Chris Spriet, Belgium
Lawrence Dunn
Sue Light of Scarlet Finders - http://www.scarletfinders.co.uk/
The Red Cross
The Cuneo Society
Chris O'Hara, a musician/composer from Derbyshire who asked for advice on poems to set to music
Clive Barrett researching Constance Renshaw
Clive Bettington of the Isaac Rosenberg Statue Appeal, London
Richard Speed and the Knitters and Natters group in Lincolnshire
Stanley Kaye and the Remembering WW1 in 2014 one hundred years Facebook Group
Mary Sky Mac
Sonia Chapman
Terry Bunn
Kathleen Holyhead
John Barnes, Chairman, Royal British Legion Club, Old Trafford Branch, Manchester
Dorothy Clare
Penelope Monkhouse from Germany
Hugh Sykes, BBC, London
Chloe Smith MP, Norfolk North
Professor Gary David Mole of Bar-Ilan University, Tel Aviv, Israel
Sally McBride, a teacher from New Zealand
John Seriot, a teacher from Norway

Michael Shankland – who is compiling a WW1 anthology
Professor Nancy Sloan Goldberg, Director of Graduate Studies, Middle Tennessee
State University
Dr. Robyn Rowland, University of Melbourne
Ken Montgomery, Head of International Affairs, YMCA
Paul Davis, Commonwealth War Graves Commission
Jana Osborne, General Secretary, The National Federation of Women's Institutes
Chris Morton – Royal Artillery Website
Terence Zuber, author of "The Ardennes in 1914"
Laura Schwartz, Warwick University
Cadbury's Bournville
Bairbre O'Hogan from Dublin, who, as a child, knew Winifred M. Letts
David Reynolds, Great-Nephew of Beatrix Brice Miller
Richard Wilson – a relative of Marjorie Wilson, poet
Roger Quin, Janet Begbie's Great-Nephew
Andrew Bomford, a relative of Nora Bomford
Tessa Tarratt, a Great-Niece of May Sinclair
Annette Shelford, Great-Niece of Violet Spender
Gillian Kirkwood, Vivien Saunders and Carolyn Kirk - Women's Golf
Pat Clare, Archivist, Abbots Bromley School
Simon Lawton of Blackpool Fylde & Wyre CVS
Duncan Hodgson of Left Coast
Susanna Forrest of http://susannaforrest.wordpress.com
Matt Jacobsen of OldMagazineArticles.com
http://www.oldmagazinearticles.com/articles.php
Rowena Edlin-White, Nottingham Women's History Group
Jen Falding, Culture Liverpool
Patrick O'Reilly and Lisa Banks, Atlantic Canadian Poets Archive
Rob Phillips, National Library of Wales
Chris McCabe, Librarian at The Poetry Library, Southbank Centre, Belvedere Road,
London SE1 8XX
Rik Sowden, a student from Birmingham University
Chad Martin of Doing Our Bit
Dr. Jane Potter, Oxford International Centre for Publishing Studies
Iola Baines, Film Development Officer, National Screen and Sound Archive of Wales
at the National Library of Wales
Theresa Saxon, Subject Co-ordinator, Literature and Cultures, School of Language,
Literature and International Studies, University of Central Lancashire, Preston
Kathrin Eckhart, Luxembourg
Will Kaufman, PhD, FRSA, FHEA, Professor of American Literature and Culture at
The School of Language, Literature and International Studies,
University of Central Lancashire, Preston
Sonia Bidwell, Textile Artist/Storyteller – www.spanglefish
Debbie Wanless PA to The Viscount and Viscountess Cowdray
Laura Maffioli-Brown and Mike Barter of the Royal Star & Garter Homes, Middlesex
Seona Ford - Chair, Dorothy L Sayers Society: www.sayers.org.uk
Christen E. Runge Assistant Curator, Art Collection Special Collections Research
Center, Lauinger Library Georgetown University United States of America -
http://www.loc.gov/pictures/collection/wwipos/
The Officers of The Gallipoli Association - http://www.gallipoli-association.org/
Richard Brodie of the Devil's Porridge Museum to the memory of the Munitions
Workers. Gretna

Letters Page, The Times Newspaper, London - www.thetimes.co.uk
Dr. Ian Olson of Aberdeen
Dr. J. Whittredge and Professor G. Dawe, Trinity College, Dublin, Eire
Professor G. Williams of Bangor University, Wales
Lt. Col. (Prof.) G.E. Visser, Department of Military History, Stellenbosch University, South Africa
Professor Dr. Shaun Viljoen from Stellenbosch University, South Africa
The Riverside Writers Group from the Wirral Peninsular -
http://riversidewriterswestkirby.blogspot.co.uk/p/anthology-2013.html
Jim Bennett of The Poetry Kit website - www.poetrykit.org
Erica from the BHSOGS for her help and encouragement
Mike Lyons for sending me a copy of his book about the Austrian Poet "Ingeborg Bachman enigma Selected Poems", Ariadne Press, 2011
Yoshihiko Makanishi from Japan for helping me find a Japanese poet
Leslie Johnson, Wirral for her encouragement
Les Voix Perdues – A Capella singers from Belgium -
https://www.facebook.com/groups/580247245389444/?fref=ts
Emma van Bijnen from Amsterdam
Stephen Cribari, a poet who teaches law at the University of Minnesota, America and the American Notre Dame Law School in London
Suzanne Raitt, Professor of English at the College of William and Mary, Williamsburg, Virginia, America
Dawn Spooner, Jacky and Rianne from Feetwood Library, Lancashire
Arnold Sumner of Arnold Antiques, St. Annes on the Sea, Lancashire
Lisette Matano of Georgetown University Library, Washington, USA
The Cross and Cockade Society
The Gallagher Family at Park's Art Deco Café, Stanley Park, Blackpool
Roger Phillips, BBC Radio Merseyside
Mrs J. Kingsland, Archivist at Downe House School, Berkshire
Sheena Gaskell and her Team at the Birkenhead Reference Library, Birkenhead, Wirral
Nelson Library, Lancashire
Roger Hull, Liverpool Records Office
Soki Kotavo, Japan for his help in finding a poem in Japanese
Dean Echenberg of www.warpoetrycollection.com
Michael Halewood of the Antiquarian Bookshop in Friargate, Preston
Daniel at Centenary News
Sylvia Wild
Dave Hollowell-Geddes of Stow Maries WW1 Aerodrome, Essex
University of Cork: Emma Bidwell and Sandra McAvoy, Coordinator, Women's Studies
Dania Ratiba of the DJ School Association, Stoke-on-Trent
Jennifer Birkett, Birmingham University
Anton Orlov – www.thephotopalace.blogspot.com
James Reaney of Sun Media, Canada
David Milholland, OCHC
Robert Langenfeld, Professor of English, University of North Carolina, Greensboro and ELT Press
Professor Brian Murdoch, Sterling University
Robert Miles, Lincoln, Nebraska
Richard S. Fogarty, Associate Professor, Department of History, University at Albany, SUNY, New York

Gregg Todd, former chairman of Deddington Library
Tim Kendall, University of Exeter
Professor Steven G. Kellman, Professor of Comparative Literature, University of Texas at San Antonio, Texas
Corinne Peniston-Bird, Lancaster University
Professor Joshua S. Goldstein, USA
Glennis McClement, The John Buchan Society
Caroline Murphy, Executive Officer, School of Languages, Literatures and Cultural Studies, Trinity College, Dublin
Roger Phillips BBC Radio Merseyside
Dr Julia Whittredge, Global Officer, Trinity College, Dublin
Bella Blisset, Beauty Editor "You" Magazine
Tom Day – University of Central Lancashire
Dr. Mark Orme – University of Central Lancashire
Dr. Petra Bagley – University of Central Lancashire
Stephen Baker of the Re-enactment Group "D" Troop Lancashire Hussars
Sally Ronchetti, Artist, The Wilfred Owen Association
Søren Hawkes, Artist and Tour Guide, Belgium
Ivan Berryman, Artist
Eric Thornton, Artist
David Scheinmann of David Scheinmann Photography
Cynthia Greenwood, Volunteer, Salford Museum and Art Gallery
Dr. Kate McLoughlin,   Reader in Modern Literature at   Birkbeck, University of London
Rebecca Bowler, Sheffield University and The May Sinclair Society
Dr Hazel Hutchison, Director, Centre for the Novel, School of Language and Literature (English), University of Aberdeen
Phil Parker of The Lightning Process
Helen James, Lightning Process Practitioner
Kath Holmes
Takis Liakopoulos, Greece
Robert Langenfeld, of ELT Press and Professor of English, University of North Carolina, Greensboro, NC, USA
Rob Phillips, National Library of Wales Welsh Newspapers Online project
Geert Buelens, University of Utrecht
Peter Appelbaum, Pennsylvania, USA
Elliott Jackson
Marie Kershaw, Ceramic Artist from Ansdell, Lytham St Annes
Helen, Paul and Anna Malindi Kirkup

FACEBOOK GROUPS
Peter G. Parsley, Belgium – Poems of Peter G. Parsley
WW1 Buffs
Clare Gervasconi and Yvon Davis of Ballarat, Victoria, Australia of the "Mud, Mining, Medals" Facebook Group
Peter Allen "Anything to do with World War 1" and "Friends of the RND and Royal Marines Light Infantry in WW1" Facebook Group
David Harrop of the "Friends of Manchester Postal Museum" Facebook Group

FEMALE POETS, INSPIRATIONAL WOMEN AND FASCINATING FACTS OF THE FIRST WORLD WAR

*Writer, poet and broadcaster
Lucy London*

"Female Poets, Inspirational Women And Fascinating Facts Of The First World War" has been set up as a small charity with constitution with the following aims:

To advance education by enlightening, informing, raising awareness of and inspiring creativity - throughout the North West of England and beyond – in works of artistic, literary, poetic and educational merit whose main subject is war and conflict, with particular but not exclusive reference to the work, life and time of inspirational people and interesting facts arising out of conflict.

And

To inspire and encourage modern day writers, poets and artists to further explore these themes and produce and display their own works.

*"One lady was in tears looking at the Female Poets.
She said she'd never seen anything so powerful in her life.."
(Wilfred Owen Story, July 2013)*

Our Exhibitions seek to inform and educate people about the 1914 - 1918 War using poetry, photographs and biographical details in easily assimilated formats such as visual exhibitions, mobile displays, printed materials, poetry readings and multimedia applications

To date, exhibitions have been held at:

The Wilfred Owen Story, Birkenhead
"Female Poets Of The First World War"
(Nov 2012 to January 2014)

Parks Art Deco Café, Blackpool
(March 2013)

The ACE Centre, Nelson
(August – September 2013)

Fleetwood Library, Fleetwood
(October – November 2013)

University College Cork, Ireland
(March 2014)

Stowes Maries WW1 Aerodrome, Essex
(March 2014 - ongoing events)

The Wilfred Owen Story, Birkenhead
"Fascinating Facts of the Great War"
(March 2014 onwards)

Materials have also been provided to Salford Museum & Art Gallery for use in their "100 Years Ago – Salford At War" exhibition, which will run from March 2014 to late 2015

Entry to exhibitions is free and is aimed at members of the general public who may not have much prior knowledge of the First World War or of poetry.

Exhibitions can be tailored to suit the requirements of the organiser, with local poets and information included where available. We can also help to organise poetry readings, writers' workshops or informative talks. If you would like to discuss the idea of bringing an exhibition to a venue near you, please do get in touch.

Exhibition materials are currently available in A2, A3 and A4 formats - as shown below - to suit your display requirements:

A2 white satin 195g paper stock – shipped rolled in a tube
A3 250g colourtech white card - shipped rolled in a tube or flat in a padded envelope
or A4 250g colourtech white card - shipped flat in a padded envelope

A full list of people and topics covered is available upon request.